RAISING UP THE CHAMPION WITHIN YOU

Lessons from the Early Life of King David

R.L. PELSHAW

Copyright © 2000 R.L. Pelshaw. All rights reserved. No part of this book may be reproduced or transmitted in any form or by any means, electronic, mechanical, including photocopying, recording or by an information storage and retrieval system-except by a reviewer who may quote brief passages in a review to be printed in a magazine, wed site or newspaper-without permission in writing from the publisher. For information please contact: R.L. Pelshaw Company, 2411 O Street, Suite 2, Omaha NE 68107, USA.

Unless otherwise noted, scripture taken from New King James Version Copyright © 1982 by Thomas Nelson, Inc. Used by permission. All rights reserved.

Published by:

Strategic Media Corporation, an imprint of
R.L. Pelshaw Co.
2411 O Street, Suite 2
Omaha NE 68107
402.932.7777
pelshaw@hotmail.com

**Additional copies available for purchase at
www.amazon.com**

ISBN: 0-9704261-0-0
Library of Congress Control Number: 00-92044

First Edition Published in the United States of America
Second Printing Published in Nairobi, Kenya 2005.

Dedication

Dedicated to the Living Memory of my great friend and former pastor
The Rev. Lester L. Jordan, Sr.
*Who in his short life taught me how to live, how to dream,
How to believe in myself when no one else would,
And who gave me the tremendous gift of being the closest thing I ever had to an earthly father. Without his friendship this book would have never been written. Les – THANKS!*

Acknowledgments

In life we meet many people. Occasionally some of those people become friends. Even more rarely, others become close friends, the kind to be cherished like precious jewels that shine in our lives. One such friend God has given me is my friend Bishop Justus Wanjala.

I cannot convey the profound love and appreciation I have for my lovely wife Cici. No one else in my life has shown me the love, respect, and encouragement that she has. More than this, she has made me strong, and has always encouraged me to fulfill my dreams.

CONTENTS

Preface   page 1

Chapter 1:   History's Greatest King?   page 3

Chapter 2:   The Fall of Saul   page 9
Chapter 3:   Knock, Knock. Destiny Calling!   page 13

Chapter 4:   Anointing –
Sweet Smells and Submission   page 17

Chapter 5:   Getting Anointing to Work in You   page 23

Chapter 6:   Give Me A "C": Calling   page 31

Chapter 7:   "P" Is For Prophetic Word   page 37

Chapter 8:   God's Personal Covenant
With You   page 41

Chapter 9:   David And Saul Finally Meet   page 49

Chapter 10:   So, Who Wants To Fight Goliath?   page 55

Chapter 11:   The Tragic Trilogy   page 67

Chapter 12:   Preparing to Face Your Enemy   page 85

Chapter 13:   How to Disarm and Destroy
Your Enemy with His Weapon   page 99

Chapter 14: Two Ways to Cause Success
              To Avoid You   page 115

Chapter 15: Dealing With Success Without
              Driving Everyone Else Crazy   page 121

Chapter 16: Success Without Bigshotitis –
              What To Do When You Get There   page 137

Chapter 17: What Have We Learned
              From David?   Page 147

Preface

Have you ever found yourself stuck hopelessly in a rut? Do you have dreams or a calling but don't know how to fulfill or realize them? Have people not appreciated your talent despite how hard you try? Have you been betrayed by a close friend or loved one? Has someone that you've helped tried to hurt or destroy you? Then you have a lot in common with one of history's greatest men: King David, a man "after God's own heart."
(I Samuel 13:14)

Throughout David's life he grew closer and closer to God's actual heart. The "heart" is your true self. So when it is said that David was "after God's own heart" it meant that David was truly like God. Romans 6:16, 19, 22 shows us the growth process to developing God's actual heart is. We begin with accepting Jesus as your Savior, receiving the unconditional salvation of God. Growth towards God's heart begins with obedience. Consistent obedience develops righteousness, which makes us like Jesus and His heart.

This study will explore how to develop the character and faith of David to become a person after God's heart. Specifically, we will learn how to use this character and faith to find God's purpose, covenant, and call for your life, and how to fight to gain them.

The scriptural texts noted, but not quoted, are provided as a reference for further study. Scripture texts that are inserted are necessary for this study, and should be read. Unless noted, all scriptural references are from the New King James Version of the Bible.

I pray that God touches you with practical revelation, motivation, application, and insight from His Word as we go through this study together.

Yet in all these things we are more than conquerors through Him who loved us.

Romans 8:37

Chapter 1

History's Greatest King?

Come with me on a journey. We will travel back 3,000 years to the rocks and valleys of Judah in the ancient land of Israel at a time when King Saul was ruling in corruption and selfishness. Once a man of great humility and a sweet spirit towards God, Saul had poisoned himself with the aphrodisiacs of power, pride, and self-gratification.

In sorrow, God moved upon His prophet and friend Samuel to anoint a new king. Samuel was not sent to a palace or a great city of known respectable men. God brought Samuel to the small forgotten wayside town of Bethlehem, to the house of a humble farmer named Jesse.

Jesse's sons were presented to the man of God, who was impressed by their appearance, not with their hearts. Out in the boondocks, baby-sitting smelly unappreciative sheep, hopelessly stuck in a dead-end job, David the youngest son of Jesse was called to come home to be presented to the prophet. David's life would never be the same again.

David is one of the most important Old Testament characters. As Israel's greatest King he ruled the kingdom for over forty years. The author of most of the Psalms, David taught a nation to fall in love with the God of Abraham, Isaac, and Jacob. Sixty-one chapters of scripture are dedicated to his life including I Samuel chapters 16 – 31; all 24 chapters of II Samuel; I Kings 1 & 2; and chapters 11 – 29 of II Chronicles. David is referenced 1,085 times in scripture.

The reign of David, regarded as Israel's golden age, was a time of peace, strength, and prosperity. All other kings of Israel and Judah were measured by how similar they were to "their father David."

David's greatest legacy

As Israel's greatest king, David united a torn country, defeated all his enemies, courageously ushered in a period of prosperity, and amassed enormous wealth. In addition to his worldly exploits, let's not forget that he had a uniquely intimate relationship with God, and he wrote a significant portion of the Bible.

David imparted wisdom, character, and excellence as a great leader and facilitator of misfits, warriors, and a nation. David knew how to lead, train, and develop skill, faithfulness, and loyalty, as well as discover a person's true potential. Yet none of those things were David's greatest legacy. So what was?

David was perhaps the most famous ancestor of Christ. With unique honor for David, Jesus was not called the son of Moses, Elijah, or Isaiah: he was called *the son of David.* We gain important truths by knowing why this was so.

The Old Testament book of Ezekiel prophesies that the Messiah would be of the lineage of David (Ezekiel 33: 23 – 31; 37: 24 - 28) and an heir of his integrity, talents, and exploits. But the people called Jesus the "son of David" because they wanted Jesus to arise and be another great military leader, like David, to deliver the Israelites from Roman oppression and restore the kingdom. Jesus was a physical descendant of David, but he was accurately called *the son of David* for spiritual reasons.

Many things in the Bible simultaneously have both a physical and a spiritual connotation. One of the deepest spiritual truths is that Jesus was and is the Messiah – the *"son of David."* Yet also in Biblical times, in the physical sense, one was known by his family parentage. If Jesus had been called the son of Moses, then the people would have believed Jesus to be a great .awgiver. If Jesus were called the son of Elijah or Isaiah, then they would have thought Him to be a great prophet.

David was a type of a king and priest (spiritual leader), and as the "*son of David*" the people expected Jesus to be a spiritual leader and a king. Although David didn't officially have the office of a priest, he did the work of a priest by teaching and leading the people in worshipping God.

Now Jesus **is** the King of Kings and our High Priest, and the One whom David's heart grew to be like. Revelation 5:10 says that God has *"made us kings and priests to our God; And we shall reign on the earth."* God has ordained us to be kings and priests as well. How to get there is the topic of this teaching.

Who was this man?

David was passionate, poetic, athletic, musical, handsome, a man's man, a fierce warrior (both physically and spiritually), and a loyal friend. Although far from perfect, his was the story of the original underdog gaining success and achievement against all odds. He overcame loneliness, depression, jealousy, hopeless situations, low expectations of others, insurmountable odds, attempts on his life, conspiracy, adultery, lust, murder, and intrigue.

In the end David had transformed a group of misfits and outcasts into "David's Mighty Men." Without intimidation or resentment, he discipled and developed this outcast group into a team of fiercely loyal men of character and integrity that were greater warriors than he. Near death, he humbly transferred his throne to his son Solomon.

David's character strengths were developed by:

His relationship with God
He maintained a committed and unconditional relationship with the Lord that consisted of regular study and meditation, as well as consistent habits of prayer, praise, and worship.

His contentment
He was content tending sheep, and serving wherever needed.

His faithfulness
He stayed with the sheep while his family was with the prophet.

His humility
He did not flaunt himself in front of the prophet Samuel, and he did not flaunt himself in front of Saul after he was anointed King.

His vision
He did not limit God by doubting that God made him king, despite when becoming king looked impossible.

His faith
He trusted God to perform what He promised.

His reputation
It was his reputation that brought him initially into Saul's court.

His integrity
David's integrity caused him to keep promises and be accountable even when there was no one to be accountable to.

His patience
He served Saul while he waited for God to fulfill His covenant promise to make him king. He did not try to advance himself. He instead waited on God.

His love for God
The Psalms he wrote are like "love letters" to God as he teaches a nation to worship God in the face of all circumstances.

His love and compassion for people
His defends Israel, and later his treatment of Saul and his family

His rcpentance
David was quick to sincerely repent for his mistakes.

Begin the journey

Come with me on a journey through David's life. We'll defeat the giant Goliath, perform in the King's court, fight battles, endure heartache and suffering, run for our life, and realize our dreams and callings.

Our journey through David's life is not an historical recitation. It is a practical guide from God's Word for discovering and achieving our dreams, callings, and destiny. We will discover scriptural principles that are just as real and powerful today as when they were learned tending the sheep 3,000 years ago.

Chapter 2

The Fall of Saul

Before we get into David's life, let's briefly look at the fall of Saul, and what David was about to encounter.

Saul was called as the first King of Israel, after the Israelites begged God for a King. He began as a humble and shy man, obedient to the Lord. Over time, Saul grew away from his spiritual roots. He became self-centered and did not fear the Lord anymore. When God made a specific command to Saul to totally destroy the Amalekites, including all of the people and all of their possessions (I Samuel 15: 2, 3), Saul disobeyed.

God never commands us to do anything that He has not already given us power to do. When He commands, the Lord wants His commands totally executed. God enabled Saul's army to have a military victory over the Amalekites. Instead of walking in total victory and obedience and blessing, they chose to try to pacify God and satisfy their lusts for worldly things at the same time.

Does that sound like something we may have done? Saul tried to justify his own covetous lust by saying that the Amalekite's treasures should not be destroyed. Saul and the children of Israel blatantly disobeyed God by destroying only the bad things and keeping all of the good things for themselves.

Saul later blamed "the people" for the disobedience. This could not be further from the truth. As people always do, the Israelites did the same things their leader did. Subsequently, they partook of the best things of the Amalekites. If Saul had obeyed God, the people would have also obeyed.

To blame "the people" for disobeying was wrong. The Israelites obeyed Saul's decree with precision. In chapter 14 of Samuel I, Saul gave a command that no one should eat. No one who knew about the decree that day ate for fear of the wrath of Saul. Saul's own son unknowingly broke the decree and was almost killed by Saul for it.

Show without substance

After the battle against the Amalekites, the people gathered to give a sacrifice of honor to God for the victory over their enemy. Samuel the prophet, who was to administer the sacrifice, was running late that day. The egocentric Saul, man lacking discipline and accountability, incorrectly thought that since he was king, he could do whatever he wanted. As such, Saul improperly took on the role of the priest, without the call, the anointing, or the relationship with God.

Saul did not understand the significance of the sacrifice. The sacrifice was meant to honor and thank God for a miraculous victory over the enemy. Saul instead had seen the sacrifice as a means to justify his greed for forbidden fruit. Saul thought that by wearing the ephod (priestly garments) he could appear religious and go through the motions of the sacrifice.

God was not impressed with Saul's show. The Lord is never impressed with any act that is not sincere or that is done for appearance's sake only. Saul thought sacrificing a few cattle to God, who owns the cattle on a thousand hills, would pacify God, therefore allowing Saul's greed.

As you know from the Biblical account, Saul rebelliously spared the life of the Amalekite king. Later, the Amalekites, who should have been totally obliterated, caused further problems for the children of Israel.

What really happened here? Saul chose to disobey God by not totally obeying God (I Samuel 15: 7 - 9). It's a trap into which we all have fallen. Through Saul's disobedience, we subtly see some of his character flaws.

- Saul was not a committed man, as he quickly lost focus of executing what God had wanted him to do.

- Saul had no accountability in his life and he was used to uncontrollably doing whatever he wanted to do to bring him pleasure. He justified his own wrong behavior, as he quickly made excuses for not fulfilling God's commands.

- Saul was not "man enough" to take responsibility for his actions as he lied in blaming the people (I Samuel 15: 24, 25). Despite being fabulously rich as king, Saul in his greed was guilty of lusting and coveting after someone else's riches.

Unfortunately, as a leader, Saul by example taught those around him his same lack of character and godlessness. He vexed the people by infecting them with his character flaws and bad habits. As earlier stated, the people always follow the behavior of the leader. More specifically, the vision and character of the leader are always found in the people.

Usually the leader, his vision, and his character dictate the tone and actions of a group's behavior. If the leader lacks character, most likely the group he leads will also. How can followers maintain a standard that the leader does not hold up?

In a similar example, because of Saul's unbelief – his own lack of vision – God could not raise up a champion from among Saul's ranks to defeat Goliath. All of the men around Saul had been infected by Saul's spiritual problems. Perhaps this is one of the reasons why God did not choose a replacement king from Saul's sons. Perhaps another reason Saul's sons would not be king may be related to God's judgment on Saul.

God could endure no more of Saul's reckless behavior, so He sent Samuel to pronounce judgment on Saul because of his disobedience. (I Samuel 15: 19 - 23; I Chronicles 10: 13, 14) Samuel told Saul that the Lord has rejected him from being king and that God had chosen another man to replace him on the throne.

Saul begged Samuel to not replace him as king. He even wanted Samuel to stand next to him so that nothing would appear out of order to the audience. Maybe if Saul had begged for forgiveness, instead of his job, there might have been a different result. But because Saul did not repent, Saul's pleading with Samuel was useless.

Chapter 3

Knock, Knock. Destiny Calling!

Now the LORD said to Samuel, "How long will you mourn for Saul, seeing I have rejected him from reigning over Israel? Fill your horn with oil, and go; I am sending you to Jesse the Bethlehemite. For I have provided Myself a king among his sons." And Samuel said, "How can I go? If Saul hears it, he will kill me." And the LORD said, "Take a heifer with you, and say, 'I have come to sacrifice to the LORD.' Then invite Jesse to the sacrifice, and I will show you what you shall do; you shall anoint for Me the one I name to you. "So Samuel did what the LORD said, and went to Bethlehem. And the elders of the town trembled at his coming, and said, "Do you come peaceably?" And he said, "Peaceably; I have come to sacrifice to the LORD. Sanctify yourselves, and come with me to the sacrifice." Then he consecrated Jesse and his sons, and invited them to the sacrifice So it was, when they came, that he looked at Eliab and said, "Surely the Lord's anointed is before Him." But the LORD said to Samuel, "Do not look at his appearance or at the height of his stature, because I have refused him. For the Lord does not see as man sees; for man looks at the outward appearance, but the LORD looks at the heart." Thus Jesse made seven of his sons pass before Samuel. And Samuel said to Jesse, "The LORD has not chosen these." And Samuel said to Jesse, "Are all the young men here?" Then he said, "There remains yet the youngest, and there he is, keeping the sheep." And Samuel said to Jesse, "Send and bring him. For we will not sit down till he comes here." So he sent and brought him in. Now he was ruddy, with bright eyes, and good-looking. And the LORD said, "Arise, anoint him; for this is the one!" Then Samuel took the horn of oil and anointed him in the midst of his brothers; and the Spirit of the LORD came upon David from that day forward. So Samuel arose and went to Ramah.

I Samuel Chapter 16

God's "headhunter"
Saul had been rejected by God as king. The Lord instructed Samuel to anoint a new king. Samuel knew that the people of Israel needed a strong committed leader that would rule with godliness and character yet he was at a disadvantage, because he was asked to seek a king among men that he knew nothing about. This was truly stepping out in faith! I do not blame Samuel for first looking at the appearances of the sons of Jesse because that was all he had to base his selection on, until the Lord confirmed his choice.

God quite often does not do what seems logical to us. What would you do if you were asked to select a new king? Would you hire an executive selection firm or a headhunter – a specialized recruiter? Would you solicit resumes and try to get someone who had a successful track record in political and military leadership? That's not how God does it. God, in His creative wisdom, often prefers to work with a "clean slate." That way He can mold the person into exactly what He wants and receive glory for doing the impossible.

Samuel was God's "headhunter" looking for a new king. But the Lord made his job very easy. There were no ads to place, no calls to make, no networking, and no interviewing. Like every other time when God leads someone into a difficult task, all Samuel had to do was simply obey and the Lord completed the work. Samuel simply went to where God led him and did what God told him.

Although not specifically stated in the scripture, Samuel may have told Jesse that he was about to anoint a new king from among Jesse's sons. Why else would Samuel say out loud "surely the Lord's anointed is before him?" As such, Jesse did not think that the prophet could possibly be interested in seeing his youngest, most insignificant son. David was not even called in with the rest of the family until directed so by the prophet.

David's heart
David's call and anointing is testimony to what can happen when you do not let the limitations or low expectations of others keep you from where God wants you to go. All his family saw in David was a lowly shepherd, not a great king.

God always creates marvelous things! To do this in us God requires obedience and a desire for excellence in everything we are and everything we do. So why did God pick David instead of his brothers who were older and stronger? God picked David as His "clean slate" so that He could mold him into what He wanted. The Lord knew that David loved Him, would obey Him, and would lead, protect, and sustain the flock of Israel.

Look at David's heart as a shepherd. While David was shepherding (or pastoring), he repeatedly put his own welfare and life at risk to protect the sheep. He constantly fed the sheep, he endured the sheep, and he led the sheep, all without an audience or anyone to show gratitude or praise. The sheep did not appreciate him or ever thank him, yet David kept on shepherding. For those of you in a ministry, business, or other leadership position, does any of this sound familiar?

God in His wisdom knew that David was the kind of leader Israel needed. It also is the kind of leader our families, churches, and businesses need today. Will you take the steps necessary to be that kind of leader for God?

In walks the manly man of God's plan
So in walks David, God's man. He is a short, good looking, bright-eyed kid that still smelled like sheep!

While reading or thinking about scripture have you ever wished you could have been a fly on the wall of the room, an unknown witness, to events that occurred in the Bible? Sometimes to develop conversation or to invoke spiritual thought, I'll ask people the same question: If you could have witnessed any biblical event, what would it be? I've been told the crucifixion, the resurrection, and one man jokingly told me he wanted to be there when God formed Eve because he had a couple of suggestions to give the Lord about women!

I personally have always wanted to witness Jesus preaching after the crucifixion to the captives for three days. That to me would have been amazing! Second on my list, though, is this event. I would have loved to witness Samuel anointing David King. Why? Do not think that all that was happening here was just a political transference of power.

In this single event we see several things going on. Yes, there was the *anointing*, or christening as king. However, that same act of christening was also *a calling* for David to be king, *a prophetic word* to David about his life, and *God's personal covenant agreement* for David's life. WOW! See why I wanted to be there!

Plug into God's Power Outlet – AC/PC Power!

I like to think that David plugged into God's power outlet, which is not AC/DC, but what I like to call the acronym "AC/PC." (**A**nointing, **C**alling, **P**rophetic Word, personal **C**ovenant). I've separated "AC" from "PC" because Anointing and Calling operate together in the present to fulfill your future purpose. Your future purpose and destiny are represented in Prophecy and personal Covenant.

David used his anointing, his prophetic word, his calling, and his personal covenant as weapons in the spiritual and physical battles and successes he faced along the path to his throne. As king, David fulfilled God's plan for his life. David needed and actively used every component of AC/PC to execute God's will and purpose in his life before and throughout his tenure as the greatest king of Israel.

As we further look at scriptural principles, we will explore what may be God's plan for you, and how to achieve this plan through God's AC/PC power: the anointing, calling, prophetic words, and personal covenant in your life.

Chapter 4

Anointing-Sweet Smells and Submission

Whole books have been written about anointing, and I can only briefly review a few major points here. The scriptural act of anointing in the physical sense was a ceremony to install or declare a person for a certain job or position. Once a person was anointed king, except for David, they usually began to rule as king.

In a similar manner today our leaders ceremoniously take oaths of office to assume a job or position. For instance we know that the President of the United States is sworn into office after he wins the election that earns him the right to be President. Once a person has been anointed, or sworn in, they are empowered or enabled to perform the office or task for which they were anointed to.

In Christian circles we often hear about a person's "anointing" as a way to describe their success or potential in a particular task or area of ministry. We think of a person that is an "anointed preacher" as a dynamic or very talented minister. An "anointed singer" can be a gifted person that can lead worship or bring people into God's presence through music.

A sweet smelling savor?
Anointing is also putting on oil or perfume. We know from the scripture at the beginning of this chapter that Samuel anointed David king by dumping a whole bunch of oil on his head and body. The anointing oil used contained myrrh, which has an odor that the Bible in numerous references indicates is pleasing to God.

In another reference Esther, along with the other virgins being considered for queen, were anointed with myrrh for six months to prepare in the hopes of being selected to marry the king (Esther 2:12). The Old Testament tabernacle was anointed with myrrh, and Old Testament priests had to be saturated in this wonderful smelling anointment before they went into the Holy of Holies (Exodus 30: 23 - 31). Mary's use of an expensive fragrant ointment when she washed and anointed Jesus' feet was a form of worship. She was unknowingly helping to prepare Him for the crucifixion (John 12:3 - 7).

We all love fragrant aromas. I bet you can think of your favorite one right now. Just like the same cologne can smell differently on each person, a person's anointing is unique and specific to them.

We "anoint" ourselves with perfumes and colognes when we prepare for something important or when we want to be attractive for someone else. In the Church we all seek anointing so we can minister with effectiveness. The question before us is this: why do we really want the anointing? Is it so we can be popular, talented, and attractive to the people, or is it so we can be attractive to God?

Anointing is important to God, because with the right "anointing" we cause God to be attracted to us. We have displeased God by using His anointing to attract friends, an audience, success, prosperity, and popularity instead of using the anointing to attract and be pleasing to God. Beware! God is a jealous God who wants His preparations used for Him, not to entice the praise or attention of a competing suitor (Exodus 20:5).

Competing suitors
Competing suitors can be anything: other people, ministries, jobs, assets, and hobbies, anything you put before God. In that particular situation, because of the depth of His love for us and the fact that He does not want to share, the Lord is likely to cut us away from what we are flirting with so that He can have us all to Himself, until we learn to put Him first. Other people may benefit and enjoy your anointing, but its primary purpose must be to glorify and attract God.

What is it that causes the type of anointing, or spiritual perfume, that attracts and pleases God? It is His Son Jesus. When He lives in us it causes us to exhibit that same pleasing fragrance.

And walk in love, as Christ also has loved us and given Himself for us, an offering and a sacrifice to God for a sweet-smelling aroma.
(Ephesians 5:2)

Now thanks be to God who always leads us to triumph in Christ, and through us diffuses the fragrance of His knowledge in every place. For we are to God the fragrance of Christ among those who are being saved and among those who are perishing.
(II Corinthians 2:14, 15)

Every person alive has fragrance that is prevalent in their life, just as everyone has unique body odor. What do you smell like – the fragrance of Christ or the stench of sin? The two do not mix, and one must prevail. It is up to you which one will. You choose the fragrance by what you allow to prevail in your life.

So if it feels like God is far away from you or that He is not sufficiently blessing or empowering your work, get rid of the stench of your sin, and send Him a little whiff of the perfume of Jesus living through you. Then see how long it takes before He leans over to smell your neck! Seek anointing, not for the praise and pleasure of people, but so that you invite the favor, fellowship, and presence of God Himself on your life.

Anointing is not required to get God's attention. He unconditionally loves everyone. Keep in mind one thing: God's Spirit was upon David after he received the anointing. Do you want a God that just loves you as a part of His creation, or do you want a God that dwells with you?

There's that 'S' word again: SUBMIT
Here's a question: Why was Esther chosen to be queen and the other virgins were not? All of the women under consideration were heavily anointed, and they all were gorgeous. They all soaked in myrrh for six months and six months in perfumes and preparations (Esther 2:12). I think that's enough time to be dripping in the stuff, and it is what I would definitely call heavily anointed!

Here's my point. **Anointing alone cannot bring success.** It didn't work for the women Esther beat out for the crown. A fragrant aroma alone is not enough. There must be substance under the smell.

Just like anybody can smell good by purchasing the right fragrance, putting on the right perfume can never take the place of a desperately needed bath. Even the most expensive perfume does not guarantee that you'll get a date with the one you want just because you smell good!

In the same way, anyone can get a measure of the anointing of God on them simply by sincerely seeking and worshipping God. But is the anointing being put on a sweet robe of righteousness or on the smelly filthy rags of sin? No matter what you do, stench and cologne do not smell good together. They actually cause a repulsive reaction.

To make sure your anointing is on your robe of righteousness, you have to repentantly bathe in the blood of Jesus and change out of the filthy rags of sin by continually crucifying that dead and rotting fleshy sin that defiles you.

Esther was chosen to be queen because the king recognized that she had all of the qualities necessary to be the perfect queen for him. Not that she was perfect, but she was everything that he wanted. There was more to her than just good looks and good perfume.

Unlike some people's anointing, there was more to Esther than just good singing, a little shouting and dancing, or good preaching. Esther was so prepared to be queen that she even appeared like what he wanted his queen to be, even before the coronation. This was the favor of God.

Even though you may have popularity, a command of the scriptures, great anointing, talent, and good looks, you still need the advice, help, and support of other people to fulfill your purpose. But that's not all. Esther had to be in **submission** for her anointing to cause her to be selected. Esther herself became submitted to the one man who knew what melted the king's butter, no one else but the king's chamberlain.

It says in Esther 2:15 that when it was time for her to be presented to the King for consideration, Esther did not request anything except what the King's chamberlain had suggested. What makes this critical for her selection as queen? The King's chamberlain knew what the King liked and disliked, and he told her exactly what she needed to do to get his attention.

Don't just be in submission to everybody or take the suggestions of everyone. Only submit to those spiritually mature people that will help get you closer than you are now to King Jesus. The other women, although equally anointed (in myrrh and perfumes) for the task, did not yield in submission to someone who knew exactly what could be done to get them closer to the king. The other anointed women undoubtedly tried to do it their way without seeking the advice or help of anyone. This is another reason to be a part of a fellowship of believers instead of going through life as the "Lone Ranger."

Esther's gift of beauty, her anointing, the preparations, and the God-given favor were necessary to get her in the palace gates, but it was her submission that ultimately got her the crown. Here is just another example of how *"many are called, but few are chosen."* (Matthew 20:16)

Just because you have great anointing, preparations, and gifts, it will be the level of your submission to God and proper accountability that will determine your success.

So what qualifications do you need for this job?
In its simplest and most practical form, I like to think of an "anointing" as a divine empowerment to perform or execute a particular talent or task. The Bible says, *"the yoke will be destroyed because of the anointing"* (Isaiah 10:27). Usually or eventually a person is very good at, or at least can easily learn, something they are anointed to do.

When someone is operating in the area(s) to which they are anointed, they will be happiest and most effective doing those things. Why?

Because there is not a "yoke" or bondage associated with executing that task.

Conversely, we will be least effective and least happy doing things we are not anointed for because there is no divine bondage-breaking power present to help. Once anointed for a skill or task, we have divine strength to shake off bondage in our areas of skill, talent, or ministry should we choose to use it.

Too many people confuse anointing as a means to get a quick fix or an instant result. Dump that oil on me now God so I can go out and do your work! Anointing alone cannot bring success to a person or a ministry. Anointing is wonderful, but anointing will never take anyone as far as solid character and consistent development will.

Chapter 5

Getting Anointing to Work in You

Character, Consistency, and the Wayward Seed

Dr. Bill Hamon in his book *Prophets and Personal Prophecy*, uses a great analogy to describe the anointing of God. He says that "anointing is like yeast that makes bread rise or water that makes seed sprout in dry ground." [i] Adding to his excellent example, working in ministry or living your life with anointing but without character and consistency is like trying to bake bread with yeast yet no dough. Have you ever tried growing a crop with seeds alone apart from soil? Both the yeast needs dough and the seed needs soil to serve as stable environments from which they can develop, grow, and fulfill their purpose.

The amount of yeast that bread can handle without being deformed is directly related to the dough the yeast is in. They must be in proper proportion to each other. Over-watering land causes erosion and even flooding which destroys crops. Over-planting seed causes undo stress on the crop and land, and is equally as counterproductive. It is possible for yeast to overpower dough and water or seed to overpower soil. If unchecked, it is possible for anointing to overpower character and consistency with the same unfortunate results.

Yeast works in the dough without you ever seeing it or knowing it's there. Yet it is apparent the right amount isn't there if the dough does not rise into a normal loaf of bread. Natural law dictates that seed grows in the soil without ever being seen until a sprout comes forth. Character and consistency must be at work in our lives whether there is an audience present or not, before we reap the benefits from our efforts. We have true character and consistency in our life when it is prevalent and operates when no one else is around to observe.

Seed is great when it is fulfilling its purpose. It is useless when it rots in the grain bin. Nobody has to tell the seed its purpose. It knows what it is supposed to do.

We are God's seed, yet we struggle to find our purpose. We jump around trying to do things we think we like, and then we lose focus. Then we try to get involved wherever there is a need, and we get burned out. All the while we are waiting for our true purpose to materialize.

To find our true purpose, we must first submit our life, heart, will, emotions, habits, thoughts, and dreams to God so that He can plant us where we will grow. Then, after stability, faithfulness, and maturity, we will bring forth fruit. But before we realize the results of fulfilling our purpose, we must be planted, and not be a wayward seed.

In the parable of the sower (Mark 4), a seed outside of soil was considered to be *"scattered by the wayside."* Common sense says that wayside seed is incapable of ever bearing fruit. Why then do we think we can productively live and minister (try to bring forth fruit) when we live our lives as a scattered seed? We do this by not having consistent character or consistent godly habits. This can include not being planted in a local church, refusing to be submissive or accountable in our lives or ministry, an inconsistent prayer life, inconsistent Bible reading and studying, and by inconsistent obedience to God's Word.

Spiritual gambling

So how do we actually get anointing from God? I think we Christians are sometimes guilty of what I will call "spiritual gambling." We unknowingly think that God's answering prayer, giving blessings, and giving anointing is like a "crap shoot." The evangelist Jesse Duplantis calls this phenomena the "gospel casino." Here's an example of how we sometimes pray or think:

> Maybe God will and maybe He won't. If my prayers work then maybe God will move. Maybe today He'll give me that

thirty-fold return. Of course now that I've shown Him how faithful and good I've been and how much work I've done for Him, He should give me that hundred-fold return that me and mama have been waiting for so long! Come on God, now I'm ready! You know we have put up with a lot of stuff and done without for such a long time. It was for you God, so now it's time for you to gimme what I want. You owe me. It's been a while since I had a really good harvest, and my time is coming soon. Daddy needs a new pair of shoes, a new car, and a new ministry too! Gimme, gimme, gimme! Come on Jesus, gimme that double anointing! Oh no – snake eyes! I didn't get what I wanted or when I wanted it. Well, we'll just have to keep plugging on. I have got to keep throwing my prayers out there. God's a good God. I'm sure someday He'll give me what I want. You know we'll be better when we make it over to the other side in that sweet by and by.

I do not mean to cheapen or demean the way people may think, pray, or seek God for things. I only used that example to illustrate in a humorous way how we sometimes act. Silly it may be, but we all have been guilty of trying to move God by "spiritual gambling" at one point or another.

The Selection, the Settling, and the Seeking
So how do we get anointing from God? Anointing is not dependent or even necessarily related to current skill, knowledge, or experience in an area. It is something that can be acquired, developed, and grown. I believe there are at least three required components for activating anointing from God. They are: Selection, Settling, and Seeking.

We know God selected David for anointing to be king because David had a quality that God wanted. David was a man after God's own heart. In Dr. Hamon's book *Prophets Pitfalls and Principles* an interesting question is asked. "Why did God anoint Jesus above all others? Hebrews tells us it is because He loved righteousness and hated wickedness (see Hebrews 1:9)."[ii] That was fine for David and for Jesus, but what do we have to make God want to **select** us?

We must make ourselves become like God in our character, desires, personality, habits, and in how we act and think. We should live our lives in such a way that we are offered up to Him as that sacrifice with a sweet smelling savor. WOW! What a tall order! We can't do it by ourselves, can we? That's why it's called "grace."

We can't just pray and ask God to change us and give us His character, and then walk around thinking it will drop out of the sky. Particularly if in the meantime we are not taking steps in our own lives to personally become like God with the strength and abilities we have.

How does God move? When we pray and seek Him, God will bless our efforts, but we first have to make an effort for Him to bless! We have to seek God's face before we find His hand.

Jesus said, *"Seek first the kingdom of God and His righteousness, and all these things shall be added unto you."* (Matthew 6:33) God wants us to worship the Creator first and far more than the creation, title, office, and blessings the Creator can bestow (Romans 1).

Elijah's mantle
Look at the relationship between Elijah and his servant/protégé Elisha. I'm sure at the time there were a great number of young men that would have loved the honor and prestige of serving God's prophet. Yet out of all of the thousands of potential candidates, the Bible gives the account that only Elisha was selected or chosen. God alone must select us for a particular gift or task.

After invited by Elijah, Elisha then had to purposely decide to follow and serve Elijah with no turning back. God asks for that same level of commitment today if we want to receive anointing from the Lord. At the time he left his father's house, I am sure that Elisha had no idea it was God's plan to raise him up as a prophet with a double portion of Elijah's anointing. Elisha had the chance to accept or reject the invitation. If he would have rejected it, then God would have sent Elijah down the road to another man.

After walking through the door of opportunity that God opened, all Elisha had to do was to settle in the process and remain obedient in his tasks at the time until God's intended purpose was manifested. By staying obedient, and without his knowledge or input, Elisha was molded into a prophet mature enough to receive Elijah's mantle.

If Elisha was not settled, then he would not have been around to be developed as the candidate for Elijah's "double portion" of anointing that was actually imparted to him (II Kings 2).

The passing of the mantle from Elijah to Elisha was not a divine right, but it was a privilege that Elisha had to work hard to receive. Elisha was settled into faithfully serving. Over time through his maturity, stability, obedience, and talents, he earned the right for Elijah to consider him as his successor.

His efforts by themselves were not enough to get the mantle to pass. Elisha still had to seek the anointing by striving for it. Elijah told him how to get the mantle, and Elisha sought to do what was necessary to receive it.

If you are asking the Lord for a particular anointing, it may be because God has birthed a desire for that anointing within you, and He wants you to seek it. Many times God will use the dreams, desires, talents, skill, and knowledge that you now possess to help bring you to His eventual selection. He can do this because He has created you for a specific purpose.

Our job is not to attempt to re-create what God has already done for us. Rather it is simply to find out what His purpose is, and to enter the process for that purpose to be activated.

A star is born?
Here's a more practical example. My friend George has a special anointing for praise and worship. He knows now that this was given by God, and the Lord repeatedly has used his gifts and anointing mightily. George did not know when he first started that God specially anointed him in the area of music.

How did George activate the anointing for music that God gave him? Unbeknownst to him, God selected him for musical anointing by giving him a desire for it, and blessing his efforts when he took steps to develop it. George just thought that he was learning music because he always liked it, yet God had deeper purposes and plans.

What happened next? Would you believe me if I told you that the first time he walked up to a piano he found God had given him such a supernatural ability to immediately be an extremely talented player and singer, that the next week he was in the recording studio cutting what became a commercially successful CD? Praise God! Well, don't believe it, because that's not what happened!

I'm sure the first time he touched a keyboard he made it clunk just like everybody else that can't play yet. Yet my friend took his desires and dreams that God placed in him and stepped out in faith and started taking lessons. Lessons and practice were the only things he knew to do to activate that gift and anointing in him.

From that point on he settled in the process and he sought the praise and worship anointing by spending a lot of time practicing, learning, and praying for God to help and bless his efforts. Back then if I told him he was stepping out in faith to activate an anointing of God, George would have said that I was crazy. All he thought he was doing was learning how to sing and play the piano because he enjoyed it! When God gave him the desire for music, He didn't tell him that he would be used to bless churches all over with his gift. If He would have told George that at the beginning, who knows what would have happened!

Is the sky falling?

I can personally report to you that George's head was never bruised by a piano falling down from heaven on him. Not even grazed. I don't believe that David's head was ever bruised or grazed by a throne dropping on him either.

Elisha didn't wait on his couch, holding a remote control, while Elijah's mantle magically floated onto his doorstep. He had to seek and stick with Elijah until he was able to be there to grab the mantle himself. If we want anointing and power from God, we are going to have to work to stay walking close enough to the gift-giver, Jesus, in order to receive the gift.

Even though the throne did not fall out of the sky, the anointing for that throne does come from God above. But the anointing is not the office! The anointing is the spiritual empowerment for you to grow into and execute the purpose God has for us. The anointing is also the spiritual aroma that attracts God's companionship. It makes Him want to be around us while we are doing something. Of course, when God is on the scene everything changes for the better!

Even this book didn't fall out of heaven on me. I didn't wake up one day thinking I could write a series of books about David. I got a desire for writing a few years ago when I was the Adult Sunday School teacher at a small church that I attended at the time.

Here's what happened to me. Instead of using the scheduled curriculum, I asked my pastor if I could develop my own original course of study. We prayed together for a while about it, and we both felt that God wanted me to develop a study on the life of David. All we did every week for the Sunday School lesson was to go through the life of David chapter by chapter, starting in I Samuel 16. We talked about its practical implications for us today. It ended up taking a year and a half to cover the life of David this way.

What's His help like?

Somewhere in the midst of teaching this topic, God gave me the desire and the ability (the anointing) to write what is now the contents of this book. It took a couple more years for me to translate that desire into a structure and a focus to start writing. But once it was God's timing for me to begin, He divinely helped me all along the way. This book is the product of several years of prayer, study, teaching, discussing, and thinking. None of which I can take credit for.

What was His divine help like? Unlike the Apostle John and the Book of Revelation, I did not get a divine visitation to tell me what to write. Rather He helped me do what He wanted done. He did not mystically come down and make words appear on my computer. A force never came and took control of my fingers to type without my knowledge or control. Nothing was ever accomplished until I started the work He wanted. I was the one who did the work that His help enabled.

Look at the last part of Ephesians 3:20. God's blessings and help, the fulfillment of your divine purpose, are *"according to the power that works in us."* The power to find and fulfill our purpose and our dreams is within us right now. The operative part is this: we have to get to work using whatever power we've got in order to receive the benefits of the "according to!"

Don't be deceived into thinking that anointing, talents, dreams, visions, gifts, or purpose will bruise us in our head while they're dropping down from heaven. To get them, we will have to obediently and consistently settle in God's process of willing obedience to Him, and then prepare and seek those things until the Lord creates the opportunity for us to grab them ourselves.

David did not crawl onto the throne with his shepherd's clothes on, and the throne did not hit him on his head while falling from heaven. So how did he get in it? At the right time, he just walked in and sat down with ease like anybody else who had earned the right to sit there.

Chapter 6

Give Me A "C" : Calling

The act of the anointing as king was also a *calling*. A calling is God's revealed personal perfect purpose for a person. It always requires a change from the present status.

David was destined to be king. That was his calling. We know this now by the success David later had as king. God does not always call us to what we want to do, or to things that we have thought about doing.

Along the way to fulfilling our purpose, God will likely make adjustments or give us a more complete understanding as we go. That is why we sometimes have to be open to the craziest ideas! The day before Samuel came to Bethlehem, if a friend had asked David if he thought he was called to be king, David might have called him crazy! Wouldn't you?

What would have happened if David did not believe his AC/PC (Anointing/Calling/Prophetic word/personal Covenant) enough to later face Goliath, or to take any steps towards the throne? History would have probably honored another man God would have selected for the tasks that were at hand.

Don't try to be something you're not. It'll kill you.
It is dangerous to try to do something that we are not called to do. What if David had not been called to rule, yet tried to be king because he thought he would be good at it? Maybe his parents always told him he would be a good king. Maybe he liked the prestige, fame, or money that being king would bring. Who wouldn't?

All of this is well and good, but if he were not called to be king, then he would have quickly met his demise, or at least been miserable along

the way. I think one of the javelins Saul was throwing around later (I Samuel 18) would have hit its target! David would have definitely been outside of the will and protection of God if he had tried to generate or activate a calling that was not God given.

Have a will to live
The greatest benefit of calling is that it is God's purpose for our life revealed to us. Having a life with purpose is a wonderful thing. Ask somebody who thinks they do not have a purpose in life, and they will tell you just how great having purpose is. So what is our purpose? In general, the answer to this question for the entire human race is found with my favorite scripture:

Let us hear the conclusion of the whole matter: Fear God, and keep his commandments: for this is the whole duty of man. For God shall bring every work into judgment, with every secret thing, whether it be good, or whether it be evil. (Ecclesiastes 12: 13, 14 KJV)

Each of us was created by God for a purpose. Maybe you have wondered what your purpose is or why you have been created. Maybe you are frustrated because you have knowledge, talent, and ability but you feel like you are not being properly recognized. Maybe you do not have anything challenging or meaningful to use these things for. The Bible says in Ecclesiastes 9:10, *"Whatsoever your hand finds to do, do it with your might."* Your problem could be that your hands have not found anything to do. What do you do then?

I just don't seem to fit
It is critically important to know, operate in, and work towards, the call God has placed on your life, no matter how big or how small the call may seem. The Bible says the body of Christ is fitly joined together (Ephesians 4:16). That means we each have a place where we belong. The problem is we all just don't know where we belong or how to get there.

Is your life missing purpose? Do you feel like you do not know if you have a calling? Do you wonder if your dreams are real goals or fantasies? I suggest that you probably have a calling, but have not realized it yet. You may already know your purpose, but you may have been running from it, been afraid to try it, or you've been slow to implement it.

Maybe you have yet to find what your dream or purpose is, but that does not mean that you have to waste time. You can take steps now to start to realize these things in your life.

Begin by honestly and completely submitting your life to God, without reservations. Seek Him in prayer, and ask Him to reveal and lead you to your purpose, vision, callings, or dreams. Ask Him to give you the grace and spiritual authority to faithfully work to attain these things. Don't just ask God to bless your agenda, but go to Him with no expectations. Be totally open to whatever He develops, no matter how different it is from your ideas. Finally, ask the Lord to give you the humility, faithfulness, and grace to properly deal with the success and blessings that will come as God answers your prayers. Continue to do these things until you hear from God.

Since nothing starts without a vision or a dream for it, I believe God will place in you desires and dreams that will eventually lead you to your purpose. We have been taught not to chase our dreams because they may seem unattainable, unrealistic, irresponsible, selfish, or even based in fantasy. You should follow your dreams if they are dealt with in the proper context of being in God's control.

Dreams are good and are necessary to change your situation. Improving your life is not selfish, it is a God-given desire. If you focus on glorifying God, that will keep you from pride and selfishness as you fulfill your dreams and purpose.

First of all, whatever your specific purpose is, it must be to glorify God. Specifically, I Corinthians 10: 31 says to *"Do all to the glory of God."* This is not just ministry, it is all things that you do in our life - our business, our job, our family, our education, anything that we touch with our hands. Remember, God will not bless what He does not control.

Secondly, God has probably already been planting dream and vision seeds in you for your purpose, but you don't know it. *"The earth is the Lord's and the fullness thereof"* (Psalms 24:1 KJV). God created the world for us to enjoy. He owns everything. We're His children. What father does not want to share everything with his children? God created a wonderful and unique purpose for you as well. So don't stifle or run away from your dreams.

Sometimes the process of fitting into your place is a painful or uncomfortable one. Maybe that is why we are "fitly" joined together because we have to work ourselves into the area where we fit best. What you are called to may not be tops on your list of things to do, but when you do what God wants you to do then you will be blessed and successful. More pain occurs when you try to force or stay in a position that you don't belong in.

Have you ever been working on a jigsaw puzzle, and try to force a piece into a place it doesn't fit? It does not work in the natural, and it doesn't work in the spiritual either. The parts of the puzzle do not have the power themselves to get into the right place, so why do we think we can get ourselves in the right place without waiting for God to move us there? When we are in God's will, then He makes the puzzle come together and the pieces easily fit without ever forcing them.

God always gives His grace for you to fulfill, enjoy, and prosper in what He has called you to do. That does not mean that everything will be easy or that your desires will be instantly fulfilled. What it does mean is that we have a God who already knows how it all comes together, and who will cause our life to be blessed and have purpose if we obediently stay in His process long enough to let Him put the pieces where they belong.

[The Lord is] Who has saved us, and called us with a holy calling, not according to our works, but according to his own purpose and grace, which was given us in Christ Jesus before the world began.
(II Timothy 1: 9)

Oo, Oo!! Choose me, choose me!

Remember that *"many are called but few are chosen"* (Matthew 22:14). Having a calling, a prophetic word, or even have anointing for a particular task or gift does not mean you will automatically jump into your new position.

Smelling good alone will not get you the date with the person you like. Having the right anointing is not enough for an office or position. Callings are conditional and can be negated by disobedience, lack of submission, or refusal to cooperate with or stay in God's plan. If you don't believe me just ask King Saul.

With God you must grow into everything, not just jump in. You have to stay in God's perfect process long enough to properly mature and develop for God's will and plan to become complete and finished in you. I have never seen a situation where you can crawl into a crown. Even Jesus Himself, the King of the Universe, grew, developed, and waited for thirty years before He was released for His three year ministry at the end of His life.

If you are not willing to stay in the process, then you will not receive the benefit of the calling. In essence, you will never be "chosen." You can put on as much perfume as you want, but what a waste if you still have to stay home when everyone else is out on a date.

Chapter 7

"P" Is For Prophetic Word

Why was David's anointing as king also a prophetic word for David? It's simple. When Samuel anointed David as king, it was a *prophetic word* because David was not yet king. David had to trust the Lord that He would fulfill the words spoken by the prophet Samuel no matter how impossible situations became.

Prophecy is simply a prediction of what is to come. If the event happens, it was a true prophecy. Certainly David did become king and the prophetic word for his life materialized. God kept His promise to David which was originally imparted and activated in him through the anointing by the prophet.

Prophecies rarely reveal all of the details of your future. Over the course of time, God can and usually does reveal more and more detail to prophecies. He never changes them, instead He clarifies, restates, reaffirms, and repeats prophecies to give more information and instruction. This occurs when it is necessary for direction or encouragement.

Was the prophecy really necessary?
Why is it important that God gave David a prophetic word? Was it necessary? According to I Corinthians 14, prophecy is an important gift given to the New Testament church. Prophecy also was an important tool manifested throughout the Old Testament.

David needed every component of his AC/PC (Anointing/Calling/Prophetic word/personal Covenant) to achieve his throne. The throne did not just fall out of the sky you know! Of course if it did fall out of the sky, wouldn't you want a prophecy to give you future warning so you could be looking up?

For a pertinent New Testament example of how to deal with prophecies I remind you of the charge of Paul to his spiritual son Timothy, found in I Timothy 1:18. Where you see a blank, I have taken out the name Timothy so that you can read this with YOUR name in it.

This charge I commit to you, son/daughter_____ , according to the prophecies previously made concerning you, that by them you may wage the good warfare... (I Timothy 1:18)

Prophecy is given for direction, for faith building, and for use as a weapon in spiritual warfare. Prophecies are also given so the recipient knows later that God was the source of the event, and it had nothing to do with them. That way, God can always get the glory.

If properly regarded, remembering God was the source of the prophetic fulfillment will help a person deal with success. Remembering the Lord will keep us from getting proud and boastful, since it was God who did the work and not us.

True prophecy is a telling of what will happen in the future, yet unseen. Does that sound a little bit like Hebrews 11:1 at work here? *"Now faith is the substance of things **not seen**, the evidence of things **hoped for** (emphasis added)."* Also Romans 10:17 says *"faith comes by hearing, and hearing by the **word of God.**" (emphasis added)*

When used in its proper context and spoken by a person with the prophetic gift, prophecy is the "word of God." The physical act of hearing a true prophecy will cause faith to develop and grow.

Prophecy certainly does not take, nor should it ever take, a more significant role than scripture. Any "prophecy" or "prophet" that does not agree 100% with the scriptures is incorrect and should be heavily scrutinized. Not everyone receives a prophetic word, but when and if you do, you can use it to build your faith and perform spiritual warfare.

David's life gives us an example of how to use prophecy to perform spiritual warfare. In the next book in this series which deals with lessons from David's life in the wilderness, we will study a time in the life of David at Ziklag recorded in I Samuel 30. David and his men tragically lost their families and all of their possessions. While doing his job to the best of his ability, the enemy came and pillaged David's city of Ziklag. They not only burned it down, but they took all of the women and children of the city.

David's men wanted to kill David. David was in despair. This is as close as any point in David's life when he could have given up when overwhelmed by an impossible task. The scriptures say that after this tragic event *"David strengthened himself in the Lord his God."* (I Samuel 30:6)

We have the benefit of the complete Bible, and all of the wonderful scriptures and promises from God contained in the Old and New Testaments. Yet at the time of David's life, only a small fraction of the body of scriptures existed. David used the prophecy and personal covenant components of his AC/PC to perform "spiritual warfare" and thereby "strengthen himself in the Lord." The encouragement came when David reminded himself and the Lord of God's prophetic word/personal covenant that said he would be king.

The spiritual warfare was a mental battle designed to cause David to lose his faith and trust in God and to become discouraged and not take the steps to recover what was lost.

Can you imagine what it was like at Ziklag to experience the reality of a mob of heavily armed grieving angry fierce men wanting to kill you? If that did not shake your faith, then I do not know what could. But David did the only thing he could do. He had to trust God to do what He said He would do. David had to look at this situation as practically as possible. Since David knew from God that he was to be king, then he could not have been destroyed at Ziklag because he was not yet king. He had to trust in the prophetic word of God, even when logic dictated the situation was hopeless.

Numerous books have been written about the modern role of prophets, personal prophecies, and prophetic issues. I will not attempt to write another here, except to stress the importance of prophecy in David's spiritual warfare to obtain his God ordained office. I highly recommend any book or tape series by Dr. Bill Hamon, Bishop and Founder of Christian International Schools and Ministries for further information on this topic.

Dr. Hamon brings integrity, insight, and practical application to an exceptional series of books he has written on the prophetic. The titles in his prophetic series are: *Prophets and Personal Prophecy; Prophets and the Prophetic Movement;* and *Prophecy – Pitfalls and Principles.*

Chapter 8

God's Personal Covenant With You

Incline your ear, and come unto me: hear, and your soul shall live; and I will make an everlasting covenant with you, even the sure mercies of David. (Isaiah 55:3 KJV)

A personal covenant is God's promised plan for an individual. The personal covenant can be given in a prophetic word, and often the two are interchangeable. By nature of it being an event that has not occurred yet, the personal covenant remains prophetic until it actually happens.

A covenant is a powerful contractual agreement that we see repeatedly throughout the scriptures. I do not mean to cheapen the value of a covenant by equating it to a contract, but I use the comparison so we can understand its meaning in a modern context. The difference between a contract and a covenant is that a contract, although an agreement, can be broken. A covenant is an agreement so profound it is to be unconditionally performed unto completion or death, whichever comes first.

Parties to a contract or a covenant have something to perform or execute in order for the agreement to be activated. In God's covenant with the world, Jesus died on the cross and rose again from the dead to execute the fulfillment of the agreement. Yet to receive and maintain a relationship with God (the benefits of the covenant), we have something to perform. We must first repent and receive Him. Then He demands that our sinful nature die so that we might enjoy abundant life with Him.

Father Abraham
We know God had a covenant (and prophetic word) with Abram (later known as Abraham) that he would be the father of many

nations. (Genesis 17:4) God asked him to leave his homeland and go to where He would lead. Abram did not have the luxury of deciding in which country God would fulfill His covenant. He had to go where God wanted him to go in order for the Lord to contractually perform. Then God asked Abraham to seal their covenant with circumcision.

We know that circumcision was the act that symbolized the Abrahamic covenant between God and the Jewish people. In more direct terms, circumcision represents a man's intimate and personal covenant between him and his God. When a man was circumcised he was irreversibly committing to serve God to his death. Remember covenants were agreements that were to be performed to completion or to the death. When you are in a covenant, you are so committed it's not a job, it's your life. There certainly is radically different behavior when your heart is in it.

Yet if over time Abraham had not done what God asked him to do, there would have been no contract for God to honor, and we would have never heard of Abram. We all would know whoever the second choice may have been.

Remember again – *"many are called but few are chosen."*

In the course of this exchange with Abraham, God even asked Abraham if he would be willing to sacrifice his own son Isaac to prove his love and obedience for God. Abraham proved his love and friendship for God was more important than the gift and ministry that God gave, and God stopped him before he killed his son.
(Genesis 22)

Quick draw McGraw
How quickly do you perform your contractual/covenant obligations with the Lord? How quickly do you act on His voice or His proddings? I am not asking if you eventually obey God. I am wondering how long it takes you. If Abraham was not quick to obey, the Lord might have had to miraculously raise a slain Isaac from the dead!

At the time of the writing of this book, a few blessed people had purchased Internet Stocks at very low prices. Quickly in some cases, their stock prices multiplied hundreds of times greater than the original purchase price. There were real occurrences of a $5,000 investment drawing a value of $250,000 in a year. There was a small window of time for some people to purchase stocks that made them overnight millionaires. I remember the first time I heard of the windfall profits some of these people received from nominal initial investments.

Later I asked God, "Why didn't you tell me about it? I would have bought some, and then I would have been greatly blessed too." The Lord gave me a response that lovingly hurt and motivated at the same time. He reminded me that it sometimes takes a long time for me to be obedient to His proddings. Maybe if I had a track record of faster obedience, God might have trusted me with the investment advice.

My practical experience with contracts
My professional background is that of a businessman. I am a commercial real estate developer and broker, and I also owned a small chain of laundrymats in the Midwestern United States. Much of what I do is based on contracts.

If we acquire a property or a store, for instance, we do not invest anything in it until the contracts have been solidly agreed on and signed by both parties. If there is a problem or a discrepancy, we look to the contracts for guidance and problem resolution. After the property is ours, we pour everything necessary into it to improve it and create what we want.

What we want is a profitable business that we can feel good about owning and operating. What we own is a reflection of us. Sometimes I'll visit our stores and they're not as clean as we want them to be. I'll meet with my staff to remind them that people we know and respect use our facilities. If the store is dirty, then it makes us look bad.

Why? Because everyone knows we are the owners, and the stores are a reflection of us. We want our business to appear as professional as possible, because then we are not embarrassed. If we paid for it, if we own it, it is going to be what we want it to be.

Unlike God, I have never bought and paid for anything in advance of having an agreement to possess and control it. I certainly would never pay for something until I owned it. Imagine remodeling a building I didn't own.

I have done real estate deals where the client was very serious about acquiring a particular property. So serious they would offer the full list price in cash to make sure they were able to get what they wanted. In my entire successful career in real estate I have never seen someone not only offer full price, but pay for it in advance of knowing whether they owned it or not.

Yet that is exactly what the Lord did for you. He bought you and your covenant in full before He even closed the deal. Why? Because He wanted you so badly.

Have I got a deal for you!
Our contracts have always governed the acquisition of inanimate things. Jesus Christ contracts to buy living beings. He contractually, through His blood, bought and paid for the sins we commit and the blessings He wants to give us, in advance of us even knowing if we wanted His deal. This is not a license to do what we want.

The price Jesus paid was so that when we choose to enter into a covenant relationship with Him, we can enter into the "deal" knowing that He has already paid for His end of the bargain.

And what a bargain it is! All He asks of us is to bring our sins, and then He will make us totally pure. Such a deal, I tell you! He has already paid for this, and a whole slew of other things. It just gets better and better! Bring Him a life burned out, and He will make it beautiful. Bring Him tears, and He will make it joy (Isaiah 61:3).

How does this occur? It's not a matter of a one time prayer, and then waiting for Him to "zap" you. It is about developing a personal relationship with God Almighty by consistent obedience that will bring you through the process of how Jesus exchanges our sins for His beauty. The Lord's process will also cause your AC/PC (Anointing/ Calling/Prophetic word/ Personal Covenant) to be materialized.

I believe disobedience to the Lord is the very reason why some people do not receive answers to their prayers. They ask God to perform His part of the covenant, but they neglect to do what God wants them to do.

Answered prayer is neither conditional nor earned. What I am saying is that as Christians, to receive and activate the promises of God, we have to be obedient to the Lord. It was true with Saul. His disobedience cost him the kingdom. Imagine what consistent obedience would have brought him.

We know though in most contracts, you have to constantly maintain a performance level to receive the contractual benefits. In other words, we have to uphold our end of the agreement. In God's agreement, all we have to do is obey Him to uphold our end of the deal.

Yes, but have you read the fine print?
Look again at the scripture at the beginning of this section.

I will make an everlasting covenant with you, even the sure mercies of David. (Isaiah 55: 3 KJV)

What are *"the sure mercies of David?"* Every time David made a mistake and did not keep up his end of the bargain, David would repent and God would restore him to his pre-offense position as if the mistake never occurred. There were consequences to his sin, but he was always able to be restored to fellowship with the Lord.

Acts 13: 33 - 36 discusses the *"sure mercies of David"* in relation to the resurrection of Jesus from the dead. The "sure mercies" were that God would not let Jesus stay down in the ground for long. Your "sure mercies clause" is that the Lord will not allow you to stay down either. When you are low, in a rut, without answers or direction, overwhelmed, overpowered, or at the end, Jesus will lift you up just as the Father lifted Him up.

The "sure mercies clause" in God's contract is a provision in case, or I should say for when we fail. Not that God stops caring if we stop obeying. Rather, He has a provision for dealing with our failures as we grow in spiritual maturity and consistency. Thank God our agreement has a "sure mercy clause" in it! I know I have used it more times than I could count in my lifetime.

When you can look at the "big picture" it is easy to obey God. The "big picture" is that the price God paid for our covenant with Him not only allows us to have direct personal access to Him, it also makes us a joint heir with Jesus of all things to be inherited from God the Father (Galatians 4: 7).

God does not ever lead His people to a place that is not ultimately far better than where He got them from. He is trying to bless us and help us, but often we block the move of God in our lives by not consistently following or allowing God's plan and purpose for us.

God gives personal covenants directly to people. He did with Abraham. Sometimes God will use a prophet or spiritual leader to relay a covenant. Other times He will directly tell or impress upon a person the personal covenant for their life.

Does God have a covenant for unbelievers?
God even has a covenant for those that do not yet know Him. That covenant is found in Isaiah 1: 18-20:

"Come now, and let us reason together," says the LORD, "Though your sins are like scarlet, they shall be as white as snow; though they are red like crimson, they shall be as wool. If you are willing and obedient, You shall eat the good of the land; But if you refuse and rebel, you shall be devoured by the sword"; for the mouth of the LORD has spoken.

Look at the first part – "come now." God is inviting us just as we are with no conditions or expectations, no requirements to show up when you have conquered that habit or become a better person. It says exactly what it means: "come now." Then the Word says *"let us reason (*or negotiate*) together."*

What do we have to offer God that He would want to trade for? If you ask Him, He will take your sins, as deeply stained as blood on virgin wool, and He'll exchange them for a life of forgiveness, purpose, and blessing. Such a deal, I tell you! Why? Because He actually honestly totally loves you with no strings or conditions attached.

He loves you so much that He put His all on the "table" when He sacrificed his perfect sinless Son Jesus so that you could come into fellowship with the Father of the Universe. God asks for an even trade – He'll give all that He has for all that you have.

This scripture lays out for those that do not yet know Him how to receive God's covenant *"If you are willing and obedient...."* If you do not know the Lord as your Savior, you come to Him by praying out loud or in your heart, just talking to Him like He is a close friend having coffee with you in your kitchen. You tell the Lord that you are sorry for your sins and your mistakes, and you tell Him that you are coming now to receive cleansing from your sin. Invite Him to come into your heart and life as an intimate friend, and ask Him to draw you into a close relationship with Him. He will, too!

To have a great and intimate life with God, you have to let Him be your Lord as well as your Savior.

What about the covenant for those that know Him already?
The covenant for those that already know Him is found in III John, verse 2. *"Beloved, I wish above all things that thou mayest prosper and be in health, even as thy soul prospereth." (KJV)*

God isn't trying to deprive or punish you. He's trying to get you to a place where He can bless you. But it's all up to you. Your prosperity and health, according to this scripture we've just cited, is tied to how your soul prospers in God. Not that bad things won't happen, whether you do good or not. But when bad things do occur, you will be in fellowship with the Great Shepherd: the One who will lead you through.

I know that we do not always honor all of our commitments, but what about God? Is there any chance that He will not perform all that He has promised?

My covenant I will not break, Nor alter the word that has gone out of My lips. (Psalms 89:34)

God's covenants are sealed in death with the blood of His Son Jesus. They are guaranteed in the risen life of Jesus. The Lord's covenants and promises can be used in spiritual warfare to give faith, encouragement, and direction to you when the enemy attacks or when situations look hopeless or impossible.

The fact of the matter is the entire Bible is God's covenant with you, and all scripture is profitable *"for doctrine, for reproof, for correction, for instruction in righteousness, that the man of God may be complete, thoroughly equipped for every good work."*
(II Timothy 3: 16, 17).

The Bible truly is an alive book with pertinent modern applications whose truths and principles are sharper than any two-edged sword!

Are there strings attached?
The initial receipt of covenants are not conditional, except that it is up to the recipient as to whether they want to engage in the agreement to begin with. The activation and benefits of a covenant are conditional. Like the earlier scripture says you must be "willing and obedient." So, as the cliché goes, "the ball is in your court." Now, what do you want to do with it?

Chapter 9

David and Saul Finally Meet

But the Spirit of the LORD departed from Saul, and a distressing spirit from the LORD troubled him. And Saul's servants said to him, "Surely, a distressing spirit from God is troubling you. Let our master now command your servants, who are before you, to seek out a man who is a skillful player on the harp; and it shall be that he will play it with his hand when the distressing spirit from God is upon you, and you shall be well." So Saul said to his servants, "Provide me now a man who can play well, and bring him to me." Then one of the servants answered and said, "Look, I have seen a son of Jesse the Bethlehemite, who is skillful in playing, a mighty man of valor, a man of war, prudent in speech, and a handsome person; and the LORD is with him." Therefore Saul sent messengers to Jesse, and said, "Send me your son David, who is with the sheep." And Jesse took a donkey loaded with bread, a skin of wine, and a young goat, and sent them by his son David to Saul. So David came to Saul and stood before him. And he loved him greatly, and he became his armorbearer. Then Saul sent to Jesse, saying, "Please let David stand before me, for he has found favor in my sight." And so it was, whenever the spirit from God was upon Saul, that David would take a harp and play it with his hand. Then Saul would become refreshed and well, and the distressing spirit would depart from him. (I Samuel 16: 14-23)

I'm all out of anointing now. Can I borrow a cup of yours?
"*My Spirit shall not always strive with man.*" (Genesis 6: 3) Saul learned the meaning of this verse the hard way. God's Spirit departed from Saul because his own disobedience nullified his relationship with God and he had no more anointing left. His defiance cost Saul his throne and altered his own AC/PC (Anointing/Calling/Prophetic word/Personal Covenant).

Saul's closest advisors knew that God's presence had left the king, yet they did not counsel him to take steps to restore his walk with God. Rather, in their own lack of character, they counseled Saul to find an anointed person to entertain him. Instead of seeking anointing in his own life, Saul tried to use the anointing of another to make himself feel good. David would worship God in Saul's presence, and the Spirit of the Lord would come. Saul was leeching off of David's anointing for praise and worship for his own comfort and entertainment.

Saul used David's gifts and anointing *to replace the anointing lacking in his life.* All Saul received was comfort. He had no further move from God in his life because he sought his own pleasure and will above that of God's plan.

Sometimes we use TV preachers as a substitute for going to church, or to get a "zap" to feel good. We may seek pastors, prophets, or spiritual leaders so we can get direction in our life without having to seek God ourselves. You can enjoy somebody's anointing, but it will never substitute for having a personal relationship with God or for getting things right with God yourself.

Was David wrong to let Saul leech from him?
Saul would become refreshed because David was an anointed praise and worship leader, and Saul was benefiting from the anointing flowing through David's praise and worship to God. Was David wrong to let Saul benefit from his anointing and gift? No, because David was operating in an area where he was skilled and gifted.

You cannot control why a person is letting you minister to them or what they do with your ministry. You can only do what God has gifted or anointed you to do.

David did not compromise his integrity when he allowed Saul to use him for his gifts. Why should David apologize or hide from what God had blessed him with? David could not control nor be responsible for the error of Saul's motivations. David was simply there to serve as he should have been.

Yes, but why did he pick me?
God's plan is perfect. Shortly after David is anointed king, he is called into Saul's court. It was God's will for him to be there. God used David's reputation as a skilled player and a valiant man to bring him before the king. It was the anointing and gifts properly and faithfully used that gave David his reputation.

When David received his AC/PC he did not wait for God to give him an honorable title to start acting honorably. David knew he must behave honorably to achieve the honor needed to be a candidate for promotion into his true purpose.

A good name is rather to be chosen than great riches, and loving favour rather than silver and gold. (Proverbs 22:1)

It is important that we as Christians endeavor to guard our reputations as an integral part of fulfilling the AC/PC in our lives. In his instruction to Timothy, Paul laid out this requirement for those seeking a leadership position:

Moreover he must have a good testimony among those who are outside, lest he fall into reproach and the snare of the devil.
(I Timothy 3:7)

Guarding from behind (a.k.a. I got your back)
The scriptures cited at the beginning of this chapter state that Saul *"loved David greatly, and he became his armourbearer."* I believe God brought David into Saul's court to train David in the practical day to day aspects of ruling a kingdom and directing a militia. David was brought close to Saul to learn how to be a king and to train and lead soldiers.

Although not stated in scripture, could it have been God's original plan to let Saul smoothly transition the kingdom to David? Unfortunately, Saul was running from the plan of God, and Saul's consistent disobedience created and enabled his chosen path of destruction. This paved the way for the armor bearer to become the king. Talk about upward mobility!

Among other important duties, armor bearers protect and sustain the life of the dignitary they are guarding. David was so committed to his task as armor bearer that he continued protecting Saul's life even when Saul was trying to kill him.

We get upset and resentful when someone says something unflattering about us. How do we react when someone opposes us, even if that is someone you serve or love? Do we give up on trying if they gossip about us? How should we carry ourself when we work for a resentful boss, even when we are more competent than he? How will we act if someone does not pay us what we are owed? What do we do when we are treated unfairly?

So you want to be king? Are you willing to be the armorbearer to the rascal you know you are to replace, or are you too good for that?

So what is the job of an armor bearer? Terry Nance's best selling books *God's Armorbearer, Book I – How to Serve God's Leaders* and *God's Armorbearer, Book II - Bloom Where you are Planted* answer this question from a biblical and practical modern perspective. The following list is taken from chapter two of Nance's first book. [iii] Nance states that the duties of an armor bearer are that they:

1. Must provide strength for his leader.
2. Must have a deep-down sense of respect for his leader, acceptance for, and tolerance of his leader's personality and his way of doing things.
3. Must instinctively understand his leader's thoughts.
4. Must walk in agreement with and submission to his leader.
5. Must make the advancement of his leader his most important goal.

6. Must possess endless strength so as to thrust, press, and force his way onward without giving way under harsh treatment.
7. Must follow orders immediately and correctly.
8. Must be a support to his leader.
9. Must be an excellent communicator.
10. Must have a disposition that will eagerly gain victories for his leader.
11. Must have the ability to minister strength and courage to his leader.

Nance's books, among other things, do an excellent job of establishing and reinforcing through the biblical armor bearer example how to have a servant's heart, how to fulfill your purpose, how to work together as a team, and how to effectively submit to and flow with authority.

Yes, but can I have it NOW please?

Do you remember from a previous chapter how it is impossible to crawl into a crown? This gives us important insight into God's nature and process. After David received his AC/PC that he would be king, he had to submit to God's process to activate God's revealed purpose for him. Even though he was anointed for it, God did not want or expect David to start ruling until God Himself opened the door for him to sit on the throne.

God was not waiting for David to open any doors. Yet today we receive a calling or a prophecy and we think it is immediately time to sell the house, quit the job, and do the thing that God has shown us. Often it is with detrimental results. We then blame God for bad things when we step out in the wrong timing.

Although I believe God appreciates the willingness and enthusiasm, I think He would prefer to have us stay in the process until we're prepared for His purpose. After his experience with Samuel, David still had to return to the real world of the smelly unappreciative sheep he kept.

David did not attempt to immediately become king. I believe he knew that doing the work in advance of God's timing would actually be a violation of the covenant and could negate God from performing His end of the deal.

I need to feel good

Today we have raised a nation of people like King Saul that go to all extremes to maximize their own comfort and enjoyment. We are all looking for a quick "feel good" remedy. We sit on pews week after week daring the preacher to "zap" us with good anointed preaching to make us feel good. We seek men and women of God for answers and direction, instead of seeking God ourselves. We look for entertainment from God instead of a friendship with Him. We want other people to wage war and let us collect the spoils.

Christianity is not a spectator sport! Christianity is about having a personal relationship with God. Saul could have tried to restore his walk with God but he didn't because he did not want to have to obey. Saul wanted his own will first, and it cost him his kingdom, his family, his life, and his soul. What will you let your disobedience cost you?

Chapter 10

So, Who Wants to Fight Goliath?

This chapter and the one following will compare and contrast how Saul and David faced Goliath of the Philistines. Through the different approaches of these men, we will gain life changing insight and knowledge: how not to approach obstacles and how to discover and achieve our vision and goals. Let's look at I Samuel Chapter 17:

Now the Philistines gathered their armies together to battle, and were gathered together at Sochoh, which belongs to Judah. And Saul and the men of Israel were gathered together, and they encamped in the Valley of Elah, and drew up in battle array against the Philistines. The Philistines stood on a mountain on one side, and Israel stood on a mountain on the other side, with a valley between them. And a champion went out from the camp of the Philistines, named Goliath, from Gath, whose height was six cubits and a span. Then he stood and cried out to the armies of Israel "Choose a man for yourselves, and let him come down to me. If he is able to fight with me and kill me, then we will be your servants. But if I prevail against him and kill him, then you shall be our servants and serve us." And the Philistine said, "I defy the armies of Israel this day; give me a man, that we may fight together." When Saul and all Israel heard these words of the Philistine, they were dismayed and greatly afraid....

The three oldest sons of Jesse had gone to follow Saul to the battle. The names of his three sons who went to the battle were Eliab the firstborn, next to him Abinadab, and the third Shammah. David was the youngest. And the Philistine drew near and presented himself forty days, morning and evening. Then Jesse said to his son David, "Take now for your brothers an ephah of this dried grain and these ten loaves, and run to your brothers at the camp. And carry these ten cheeses to the captain of their thousand, and see how your brothers fare, and bring back news of them." So David rose early in the morning, left the sheep with a keeper, and took the things and went as

Jesse had commanded him. And he came to the camp as the army was going out to the fight and shouting for the battle. Then as he talked with them, there was the champion, the Philistine of Gath, Goliath by name, coming up from the armies of the Philistines; and he spoke according to the same words. So David heard them. And all the men of Israel, when they saw the man, fled from him and were dreadfully afraid. So the men of Israel said, "Have you seen this man who has come up? Surely he has come up to defy Israel; and it shall be that the man who kills him the king will enrich with great riches, will give him his daughter, and give his father's house exemption from taxes in Israel." Then David spoke to the men who stood by him, saying, "What shall be done for the man who kills this Philistine and takes away the reproach from Israel? For who is this uncircumcised Philistine, that he should defy the armies of the living God?" And the people answered him in this manner, saying, "So shall it be done for the man who kills him."

Now when the words which David spoke were heard, they reported them to Saul; and he sent for him. Then David said to Saul, "Let no man's heart fail because of him; your servant will go and fight with this Philistine." And Saul said to David, "You are not able to go against this Philistine to fight with him; for you are a youth, and he a man of war from his youth." But David said to Saul, "Your servant used to keep his father's sheep, and when a lion or a bear came and took a lamb out of the flock, I went out after it and struck it, and delivered the lamb from its mouth; and when it arose against me, I caught it by its beard, and struck and killed it. Your servant has killed both lion and bear; and this uncircumcised Philistine will be like one of them, seeing he has defied the armies of the living God." Moreover David said, "The LORD, who delivered me from the paw of the lion and from the paw of the bear, He will deliver me from the hand of this Philistine." And Saul said to David, "Go, and the LORD be with you!"

I always root for the underdog

"David and Goliath" is one of the most famous Bible stories. Children throughout the ages from all walks of life can tell you the cute story of tiny David meeting the big bad ugly giant. But this is not kids' stuff. David's fight against Goliath gives us important revelation and application for fighting the enemies, problems, and distractions in your life through the power of God.

Bible scholars have differing opinions as to whether the "David and Goliath" event happened before or after David met Saul. My opinion is that this incident occurred after the anointing as king but before Saul called David into his court. Since David had already been anointed king, I believe he used his God-given AC/PC power to win the battle against Goliath spiritually, and he let that victory manifest itself in the physical realm. Also, most of the Biblical account of David follows chronologically, and I believe this chapter is not an exception.

I Samuel 17 begins with David's father Jesse sending his youngest son to the battle front with some goodies for his older brothers. David had no idea that while there he would be used to conquer an impossible situation.

Sometimes we do not understand how or why God opens or closes the doors He does. But God is truly in control, no matter where we are or what we do. It is God who sends us out onto the battlefields as well. This is one way God uses to slip us into the part of the puzzle we belong in being "fitly joined together."

How much does this job pay?
At the front David witnessed firsthand the humiliation Goliath was causing the army of Israel. The army of Israel was in battle array, ready to fight the Philistines. But instead of just an army, Goliath showed up to scare and paralyze the Israelites. When he arrived, David discerned that Goliath was doing more than humiliating Saul and his army. Goliath was defying God Almighty Himself. David also heard firsthand that the champion of Goliath would be given wealth, would earn tax exemption for his family, and would marry the king's daughter.

I do not believe David's primary motivation was for his own gain, although he was entitled to the promised pay. Remember the verse *"muzzle not the oxen which treadeth the corn."*
(Deuteronomy 25: 4 KJV)

Today we get upset if our pastors make too much money or if a famous preacher has an expensive car. No one was upset when David killed the giant. I doubt anyone Jesus healed through Benny Hinn's ministry could care less how much Benny's car cost.

We will find out a little later that Saul did not keep his promise. Saul never rewarded David for defeating Goliath. David put his life on the line to earn the reward which Saul stole from him. Yet today, we have great men and women of God who fight Goliaths for us, and we fall into one of the sins of Saul when we do not allow, or we despise, proper recognition and rewards for battles won.

Jonathan: Why didn't he fight the big bad ugly Goliath?

Take a moment now to read and familiarize yourself with the account of Jonathan, Saul's son and heir, and what he and his armor bearer did to the Philistines in I Samuel 15.

Here Jonathan unselfishly steps out by faith in God along with his armor bearer. Alone and without an audience, they subdued an entire garrison of the Philistines themselves. Their efforts initiated the momentum the children of Israel needed to go and conquer the rest of the Philistines.

Jonathan and his armor bearer were just two people against an entire army. That in itself is a greater feat than David's one-on-one confrontation with Goliath. Yet history is kinder to David, even though he did not have as difficult a challenge as Jonathan.

Jonathan was used by God to bring a great and unexpected victory to the camp. This scriptural account proves that Jonathan knew how to get a vision of victory and how to take steps to physically activate that victory.

We know that Jonathan was on the scene and witnessed first hand the "David and Goliath" confrontation. I can prove this to you by closer examination.

I Samuel 18:1 says, *"When he had finished speaking, the soul of Jonathan was knit to the soul of David..."*. Who was speaking, what was he speaking, and to whom was he speaking?

David was answering Saul's questions when summoned to his tent after killing Goliath. Jonathan witnessed the whole thing, and it caused a bond to be formed. So if Jonathan was there, and knew how to trust God and let God fight the battle, why did God have to send in David from outside the camp to come and defeat Goliath? Why did God not just use Jonathan who was a proven champion?

Look closely at what occurred during and after Jonathan's astounding victory against the Philistine garrison noted in I Samuel 15. While Jonathan was out risking his life for his father and his country, King Saul made a foolish decree that everybody should fast until the battle was won.

Jonathan, after defeating the Philistines, returned and without knowing his father's decree, ate because he was famished. Jonathan was a hero and had literally saved the day. When Saul sees his son, he does not congratulate him for defeating the Philistines. He does not even thank him for risking his life. Instead, he tries to kill him for unknowingly ignoring a useless decree.

It is hard to comprehend Saul trying to kill Jonathan for unknowingly eating a little honey against his command. Maybe if Jonathan had committed treason or some heinous crime, but eating a little honey? Isn't that a bit ridiculous?

It is equally difficult to comprehend that Saul's own rules and appearance were more important to Saul than the life of his son and heir, and the nation he saved that day. The demands of the crowd of people saved Jonathan from being brutally murdered by his own father.

Jonathan learned in the most convincing and direct way that nothing he could do would ever satisfy or be good enough for his father. What father who loved his son would not be proud of Jonathan's miraculous accomplishments? Instead of praising and thanking him for rescuing Israel, Saul publicly belittled Jonathan by trying to kill him on a meaningless technicality.

Choking on success
I believe Jonathan was offended by his father's self-centered response to his victory against the Philistines. Jonathan's offense birthed a root of bitterness and resentment. (Hebrews 12: 15) This root grew and eventually choked him and kept Jonathan from ever stepping out for the Lord again. How utterly tragic to waste the potential of a great champion.

To state what happened more directly: Jonathan choked on success. Whether caused by resentment, depression, a lack of acceptance from his father, a lack of reward for the victory, or the public embarrassment his father caused, Jonathan was offended to the point that he would never make another life threatening sacrifice for his king or his country again. Jonathan's offense was a byproduct of his own reaction to success.

For whatever reason, success did not bring Jonathan what he wanted so he gave up. What he wanted was to meet a need or perhaps to please his father or his country. Any goal not rooted in a desire to glorify God or deliver God's people will leave a person with a success that is eventually empty and hollow.

As a result of Saul's response to Jonathan's great victory, great exploits were never to come from Jonathan again. Jonathan recognized that David had what he did not: the vision, drive, call, and anointing from God to be the champion for His people. If Jonathan was more spiritually mature, or if Jonathan's motivations were to help or please God, I believe Jonathan would have faced Goliath long before David arrived in the valley.

The enemy's evil seed strikes again
We see how Saul's evil behavior infected his son from doing great things and why Jonathan never again stepped out in faith for the nation of Israel or his father. Why did this disabling "root of bitterness" get planted, grow, and take hold in Jonathan?

All roots start from a seed. Remember what Jesus said in the Parable of the Sower? Immediately, after the good crop was planted, the enemy came by night and planted weed seeds right along with the good crop. (Matthew 13: 24-31) Why? The weeds were planted so that they would grow to steal and choke the life out of the intended crop.

Jonathan did not spiritually discern that his father's response was an evil seed sent by the enemy to initiate what would become a root of a destructive weed to distract and strangle Jonathan. He did not know, or probably even suspect, that the devil would use a loved one, his own father and king, to steal his vision, purpose, drive, and self esteem.

Jonathan unknowingly let the enemy plant a seed in him that would eventually steal and choke out all future vision, drive, ambition, and meaningful action. This seed developed into a root that choked Jonathan from being a "participator" into being a "spectator." Jonathan did not participate in Goliath's defeat. He was a spectator while David faced the giant.

In the case of Jonathan's success, Jonathan thought that his father's lack of enthusiasm and praise was a rejection for him and/or his accomplishments. Jonathan's mistake was in placing the praise, acceptance, and opinion of his father as more significant than the task achieved, regardless of reward or recognition.

The key is this: do not be upset or stop your efforts if the people who should thank you, be happy for you, pay you, or praise you do not do any of those things. It does not matter if it is your parents, your spouse, your boss, your minister, your congregation, or your best friend. Jesus said it best when He said, *"Take heed that you do not do your charitable deeds before men, to be seen by them. Otherwise you have no reward from your Father in heaven."* (Matthew 6: 1)

Be mature enough to realize that your victories, accomplishments, and self worth are not at all related to how people accept, recognize, compensate, or appreciate you. Never allow resentment a chance to get a foothold on your life.

Resentment is a distraction, planted by the devil, intended to keep you from your purpose.

I resent resentment

Do you have a little touch of resentment yourself? Does your boss, your friends, your church, or your spouse give you the appreciation and respect you feel you deserve?

Are you not being utilized to your fullest potential?

Does it frustrate you that you have knowledge, talent, and ability that no one will recognize or utilize?

Do people not understand you?

Resentment is something that has affected everyone at some time or another in varying degrees. Remember when you were growing up, and did not get your way? Did you ever think to yourself, "I'll just run away. Then they'll be sorry." That was a display of resentment that we hope to grow out of.

In my own life, I have been susceptible to resentment. Because of my own pride, when I did not get my way or get properly recognized, I would fall into bouts of resentment. Most of the time my resentment was caused by a lack of appreciation for my efforts. In retrospect, the things I fell into resentment over were so minuscule that I cannot even remember most of them now.

Resentment is an evil, vile element that will consume your mind, thoughts, and eventually your behavior. When I resented something, I thought about it all the time. I could not forget the hurt I was feeling, whether deserved or not. Resentment disables you from reacting and doing things the way you should.

A long time ago when I was much younger, and much less spiritually mature, I sometimes played piano for the church I attended. It was obvious that I was the better player of anyone in attendance there, and because of my pride, I was all too happy to demonstrate. When someone else did play for service, occasionally I resented it because I was the better player and I felt I was unjustly suffering for my talent. I did not recognize that I was not invited to play because I lacked the character to help minister during church service.

At first I would quietly steam. Then, when resentment started to consume my reasoning and behavior process, I gave so much thought to how I should be playing that it was absolutely impossible for me to enjoy church. Other people would observe my reluctance to participate, and it had a negative impact on the service.

Later I would fall into a "pity party" about how no one at church appreciated my talent and how I would never get to use my talents for the Lord. Shortly thereafter as a senior in high school, my resentment was manifested in a bleeding ulcer that almost perforated. I spent a week in the hospital and a year on medications because my resentment was literally eating me from the inside out.

After feeding my resentment in the midst of my pity parties, I found it increasingly easier to come up with reasons to miss church. That is when I started to become sexually promiscuous and consume alcohol regularly, unfortunately all while warming a pew!

Maybe your resentment hasn't taken you as far as mine had, but you should recognize where resentment has been a hindrance to you and stolen your peace, joy, motivation, or drive. Maybe like Jonathan it has kept you from fighting against the Goliath directly in front of you. Just because you may have fallen prey to resentment does not mean you have to stay there.

Resentment is caused by our reactions to other people's behavior towards us. Resentment often can occur when we feel we suffer for something we did not deserve. Certainly Jonathan did not deserve the treatment his father gave him.

To overcome resentment we must first have the strength to endure the suffering we receive. Secondly, we must have the grace to forgive the offense against us. If we truly forgive the offense, then we will not continue to dwell on it. It will be over and forgotten.

The Lord gave me two scriptures that helped me to overcome the effects of resentment in my life. They are I Peter 2: 19, 20 and Matthew 6: 14.

For this is commendable, if because of conscience before God one endures grief, suffering wrongfully. For what credit is it if, when you are beaten for your faults, you take it patiently? But when you do good and suffer, if you take it patiently, this is commendable before God. (I Peter 2: 19, 20)

For if you forgive men their trespasses, your heavenly Father will also forgive you. (Matthew 6: 14)

Sometimes fighting resentment is just putting up with suffering, whether deserved or not. If you do this, you will be acceptable in God's sight and not allow an occasion for resentment to afflict you. I encourage you to remind God in prayer that according to His word you are acceptable in His sight and want all of the benefits of that distinction. Watch out and see what great things start to happen for you!

do you ever feel stepped on?

Unfortunately in life we will be hurt and offended. Jesus told us that *"offenses must come..."* (Matthew 18: 7) Matthew 6: 14 talks about forgiving trespasses. The problem is, in order for someone to trespass, they first have to step on you!

Sometimes, even in your weakest moment or the time of your greatest sacrifice, someone will knowingly or unknowingly step on you and hurt you. How you react to the trespass will determine if you are acceptable in God's sight possessing forgiveness, or if you have resentment and unforgiveness in your heart.

I do not want to jeopardize the unconditional forgiveness I received from the Lord, so I will not allow myself to have any unforgiveness or resentment whatsoever. Do not resent anything, even if you feel you are justified in doing so.

Remember, we reap what we sow. If you want mercy, acceptance, and forgiveness in your life, you may have to go out of your way to sow those things into someone else's life. But nonetheless, you will enjoy your harvest.

Look at your life. Does resentment and unforgiveness haunt you? Are you held back from fulfilling your purpose and your dreams because of the disabling effects of resentment? Pray and ask God for His grace, forgiveness, and power to change your nature and to remove resentment and unforgiveness from you. Do this BEFORE you waste any more time, effort, or peace. Certainly do it before resentment chokes the life out of you.

Should I watch out the most before or after I win?
As a brief but meaningful sideline pertinent to the Jonathan situation, here is an interesting question. When does the enemy attacks most, when you are weak or right after you have won a battle? (Do not look ahead for the answer!) We know Jonathan faced a spiritual attack after his victory, but was that usual or the exception? The account of Elijah in I Kings 19 will give you the answer from God's Word.

God manifested Himself in Elijah in the most dynamic way he would ever experience in his initial earthly ministry. Elijah called forth fire from heaven to destroy four hundred prophets of Baal. Afterwards, he is threatened by an evil queen and flees for his life.

While on the run Elijah became deeply depressed. He had a pity party to end all pity parties! Elijah was not attacked with depression and fear until after he had a great victory. Before the showdown with the prophets, Elijah was not as much of a threat as he was after he killed the devil's prophets.

When you are weak, not fighting, not growing, not preparing, spectating more than participating in the fight, waiting for a champion instead of being a champion, you are not a threat to the enemy. Therefore, the enemy will likely not attack you as often or as severely as when you are a tactical threat to him. That is why we can rejoice when we face temptations and trials. The sheer nature of having an enemy to oppose you must mean that you are doing something right!

I think that is also why the Word cautions *"...let him who thinks he stands take heed lest he fall"* (I Corinthians 10:12) The time to be the most watchful is when you are strong and victorious because <u>that</u> is when the devil will attack you.

Chapter 11

The Tragic Trilogy

Funny thing about history. It is usually written by the victorious to favor victors. Of course, David was popular and had great achievements. But does history treat Saul unfairly? Why have I been picking on Saul? Saul's own disobedience removed him from the throne. But without three major errors of Saul, David would not have had to fight Goliath. Saul's actions and inactions created and enabled the Goliath situation.

By looking at Saul's faults, we learn powerful truths about leadership, character, and how to (or not to) deal with the enemy. As we review this material, keep in mind that the Philistines here represent the enemy (satan), and Goliath signifies a seemingly unconquerable problem or situation sent by the enemy.

Saul's first tragic mistake
The first mistake Saul made was to negotiate on the enemy's terms or turf. You cannot allow the enemy to tell you who you are or what you can or cannot do. Saul did not realize that when you play by the enemy's rules, and not God's, you block the hand of God from moving. You make the battle yours, and not the Lord's. Saul created the whole Goliath situation when he allowed the enemy to dictate the terms of the battle. How?

The Philistines suggested that they choose champions to fight and that the loser would serve the winner. The enemy only, and always, wants to destroy you and put you in chains of bondage. Remember Jesus' words in John 10: 10: *"The thief does not come except to steal, and to kill, and to destroy. I have come that they may have life, and that they may have it more abundantly."*

Today we have become bound to the pleasures and distractions of this world. Often the problems facing us are not sent by the devil, but are created by our own selves yielding to our flesh. We need to stop creating and enabling the Goliaths we are struggling with.

Are you having trouble resisting temptation? It is a lot easier to resist temptation if you consider that yielding to it puts another link in the chain that will eventually enslave you.

Know ye not, that to whom ye yield yourselves servants to obey, his servants ye are to whom ye obey; whether of sin unto death, or of obedience unto righteousness? (Romans 6: 16 KJV)

In my life I yielded to a particular sin so often that it became an ungodly habit – a stronghold. I had to develop consistent godly habits to break the chains of bondage and maintain the victory over sin.

Can you trust the enemy?

The Israelites through David were victors over Goliath, but the Philistines did not honor their word to become servants to their conquerors. The adversary never keeps his promise. Saul should have known that the enemy only suggests terms that bring them a position of strength and advantage, and that the enemy has no intention of ever honoring commitments.

The scriptures call the devil the father of all lies. (John 8: 44) How can you rely on anything when everything said is a lie or a poor counterfeit of the truth? Try to remember when satan attempts to entice you that the devil never tells the truth or keeps his promises. Do not believe that lying serpent when he tells you that no one will find out about that secret sin. You can always repent, but like Saul you will still have to deal with the consequences of the seed you have sown.

The Lone Ranger

Why did the Philistines send Goliath out to fight alone? It was their calculated strategy. We are in a war with satan and he uses this same strategy against us. The Philistines knew they had a man that an individual soldier of Saul could not conquer.

Like the Philistines the devil is keenly aware of the strengths and weaknesses of the army and soldiers he attacks. The enemy is always trying to get you to fight isolated from the rest of the army. That is why satan tries so hard to keep you out of church and out of fellowship with God's people.

Maybe you or someone you know has been offended and will not go to church. Maybe you are too busy with your job or your business to faithfully attend church. Beware! These are the devil's tactics for destroying you and putting you in bondage. Being in a power packed Bible preaching church and having meaningful Christian fellowship is essential to feed, strengthen, and equip the army of God for success.

If Saul had raised up and fought Goliath and the Philistines with his strength (his army), as he was supposed to as king of God's people, then Goliath's might and size would not have been an obstacle to them. Saul was not acting like the king he was. He did not use the resources available to him. It's easy for us to criticize Saul for this, but we do the same thing ourselves when we do not act like the conqueror God intends for us to be, or when we do not use the resources available to us.

What are our resources?
- The whole armor of God (Ephesians 6: 13-16)
- God's Word (Hebrews 4: 12)
- Prayer: Individual, In Agreement, Intercession, In the Spirit (Ephesians 6: 18; Romans 8: 26; Mark 11: 22-24)
- Fellowshipping with other believers (Proverbs 27: 11)
- Your testimony (Revelations 12: 11)

It's a little late to close the gate AFTER all the animals left
Did you notice in the beginning of I Samuel 17 where the Philistines were when these confrontations were occurring? They were encamped in land belonging to Judah. At the point of this showdown the Philistines had already invaded and possessed a portion of Saul's territory before Goliath was sent out.

Saul should have prepared and protected his borders before the attack that he knew would eventually come. At least Saul should have realized that a Philistine invasion was imminent. Saul could have sent spies to observe that the Philistines wanted to invade. Instead Saul waited to react to a crisis rather than preparing for his enemy.

The scriptures say for us to *"Neither give place to the devil."* (Ephesians 4:27 KJV) That means to not give him an opportunity to invade your territory – your life. If you know the enemy will attack you in a particular area where you have weaknesses, take control of the situation by strengthening your borders in advance of an attack that you know will eventually come.

More depressing than a Greek tragedy

The most tragic part of the situation facing Saul was that he had all of the power and might to subdue the enemy, but he did not know how to use the strength God had already given him. He could have walked in the power from God that would have enabled him to conquer his foes.

Today we have all of the promises of God and power from the Holy Ghost, wonderfully anointed preachers and teachers, books, tapes, Christian TV and radio, and yet we stand aside and play with the enemies and obstacles in our life, when we should be conquering and living victoriously.

Do you know how to use the strength God has already given you? Do you know how to really submit your will to God? Can you trust God to deliver you in impossible situations? Can you hang onto a promise of God long enough to receive victory or to fulfill purpose?

I challenge you to walk in the power and position God has already ordained and enabled YOU to walk in. All Saul had to do was be obedient to God, trust His promises, and he could have won battles, both on the battlefield and in his heart. Yet he chose the path of least resistance and maximum comfort.

The tragedy continues: Saul's vision problem
Saul's second tragic mistake was that he lost his vision of victory. The loss made him impotent to fight against Goliath. Nothing is ever accomplished without first having a vision for it. That is why we speak to those things that are not as though they were. (Romans 4: 17)

God's plan is for us to get a vision of victory. Get a vision of the business you want to start; get a vision of the house you want to buy; get of a vision of the career you want to have; get a vision for the education you want to earn; get a vision for the ministry you want to perform; get a vision for the people you want to help. Whenever God does something through one of His children, it always starts with a vision. If there is no vision, God does not move. You don't move either. Then things stagnate.

Saul's vision was not for God's will. Saul was consumed with making himself look good and satisfying his own selfish desires. His vision was out of focus and needed severe correction because Saul's vision was focused on himself, not on doing God's work. The consequences were that the Israelites lost power and focus because their leader lost vision. Their weaknesses were exposed and they were embarrassed.

Why didn't Saul have a vision for conquering Goliath? Certainly a large part of his problem was that he focused on himself and his problems more than focusing on God. Perhaps Saul did not know how to trust God for the victory. I wonder if Saul started to believe the lies that Goliath had bellowed at him for the forty days he presented himself. Maybe Saul realized that in his disobedience God may not move for him.

When you know you are outside the will of God it is easy to develop paranoid thinking that every bad thing happening to you may be a judgment from the Almighty Himself. At this point Saul only knew that in his own natural strength he was helpless. This all occurred because Saul and his camp did not know how to focus on God instead of themselves or their problems.

Racquetball, anyone?
I love to play racquetball. I've played since college and unfortunately, I really haven't gotten much better at it. After watching me play, friends have asked if I'm masochistic – enjoying something that tortures me. Yes, I frequently lose. But racquetball is better than tennis because in tennis you have to run too much. In racquetball, if you're like me, you can plop yourself in the middle of the court and eventually everything comes to you. Sometimes I play by the "seven foot rule." That's when I don't try for the shot if it's more than seven feet from me.

OK, maybe I'm exaggerating a little bit. I like to play and I am an average player. What frustrates me is when I miss simple shots that I have made a thousand times before. I was playing a friend of mine who was thoroughly beating me, and I asked his advice. He told me something that I already knew, but inconsistently applied. He encouraged me to keep focused on the ball before and during the shot through completion.

I tried it, and do you know what? When I stay focused on acquiring and following through the proper functions, watching and hitting the ball, I almost always get my shot. When I consistently focus my vision, even though I certainly do not possess any sophisticated playing abilities, I usually win.

Keep focused in the right direction
In racquetball you focus on the ball. For sustained success in your life, you focus on the Lord and executing the tasks He gives you. Focus on God so that you can let God fight your battles for you. Our Lord is a winner!

I am convinced that we receive what we focus on. Do you want to conquer the flesh, a stronghold, a bad habit, or even sin? Stop worrying about anything other than focusing on walking in the Spirit. This is developed by developing a life of consistent godly habits.

Walk in the Spirit, ad you shall not fulfill the lust of the flesh.
(Galatians 5:16)

Focus on getting Jesus inside you - His nature, His personality, and His thoughts. **Jesus is the true champion within.** We need to learn to let Him shine through us and fight our battles through us.

Did you know all of God's battles for this present age are already won? That's why the Father is sitting on the throne in heaven. Unlike His children, God is not out running around the universe trying to put out fires, bouncing from crisis to crisis. He is sitting and waiting for His Body – *His Church* – to arise and assume its position of kingship and priesthood!

What is a king? A king has absolute authority over his kingdom. Maybe you don't feel like a king. Is your life in turmoil or out of control? Do you feel like your throne is a long way away? Maybe you haven't a clue on how to get your throne – your dreams, your vision, your purpose. Then you have something in common with David. No one was further from the throne than he.

We learn from the life of David how to become a king. The first thing you must do is to have your vision focused on your goal and purpose. Then remain obedient to God.

God had to raise up a champion outside of Saul's ranks because all of Saul's men were infected with Saul's vision and character problems. A champion was needed who had the proper vision, that of not allowing the enemy to harass God's people anymore and conquering the enemy putting him to flight. It was the vision of bettering his life (remember the promised bounty for killing Goliath) by skillfully completing a work, whether or not he got the pay or recognition he deserved. That vision of using what the enemy attacks you with to destroy your enemy. That vision of giving God the battle to fight. That vision of raising up the champion within you.

The Lord is waiting for you to allow the ultimate champion, Jesus, to get inside you so much that He lives and fights through you. Jesus is the only undefeated Champion of the Universe.

What happened to all of my sheep?
There are a lot of great pastors and church leaders losing their flocks because there is no vision left. There is no burden for the lost, no push for growth for the kingdom of God. There is no quest for the power of God in their life or in their church, no thirst for righteousness. They are content being a spectator while another champion goes to fight the Goliaths.

Like Saul's army, they run quickly when it comes time to collect the spoils of war! But Christianity is not a spectator sport. These same pastors and church leaders with no vision wonder why their people have neither power nor victory in their life.

Sadly, these well meaning pastors and leaders do not realize they have infected their flock with the same lack of vision they have. I believe that is one of the reasons why the scriptures say, *"Where there is no vision, the people perish...."* (Proverbs 29: 18)

Am I trying to tell every pastor or leader to start a new ministry or a new building program? NO! What I am doing is to challenge you to get God's vision for life, which is to victoriously conquer the Goliaths now troubling you, your flock, or your city.

If you are in a visionless church give serious consideration as to whether or not you should attend another fellowship. Do not just change churches immediately and do not bounce from church to church either. Give the matter to God in prayer, and pray for your current pastor and church leaders. It may be that Jesus wants you to stay there to help change the atmosphere.

If you are not being fed; if you are not a meaningful blessing; or if it is increasingly difficult to enthusiastically participate then I would suggest prayerful consideration to changing to a church that has a pastor (shepherd) with a vision that you can support. A church that will help challenge, empower, and direct you to the fulfillment of your AC/PC and your dreams. You don't need to look for a "good church." What you need first is a good pastor. You usually find them in good churches.

You know how you will sin before it happens, don't you?
How do you know what to guard from attack by the enemy? Stand on II Corinthians 2: 11 *Lest Satan should take advantage of us;* ***for we are not ignorant of his devices.*** (emphasis added) You don't need me or an angelic host to tell you what your weaknesses are. Just use the brain God has already given you.

For instance, if you know that you have a particular weakness of lust or sexual sin, then do not subscribe to the cable movie channels that show filth. Do not linger at the checkout stand eyeballing the magazines with revealing pictures. Do not let your mind and your eyes imaginatively wander or gaze too long at a specific person or their appearance. Do not "accidentally" go out of your way to drive by the part of town where prostitutes frequent. Does this sound too hard? This is just a practical example of crucifying your flesh, which is what we are commanded to do. (Galatians 2: 20)

Crucifying your flesh and being totally submitted to God starts when you remove anything in your life and your actions that would expose you to temptation. In the Lord's Prayer, Jesus taught his disciples to pray "*...lead us not into temptation, but deliver us from evil: For thine is the kingdom, and the power, and the glory, for ever. Amen.*" (Matthew 6: 13 KJV)

If you do not crucify your flesh, remove potential obstacles, and stop yielding to temptation, you have already invited the enemy into your territory, and soon you will be facing a Goliath of your own. Then you will cry out to God, after you eventually sicken of continually facing the same enemy day after helpless day. Why wait till then?

Deep down you know the devices, strategies, temptations, and possibly even the people the enemy will use. You know your weak spots. Take preventative measures now to strengthen your spirit, crucify your flesh, and remove potential stumblingblocks. Then and only then will you be able to defeat the enemy and continually walk in victory. Know your own boundaries and guard your own borders.

The ironic thing is that you know while you are doing those things you are flirting with your weakness! If you do not "protect your borders" you will live your life continually running from emergency to emergency. You will feel like you are constantly under attack by an invading force.

If the Philistines had been stopped at the borders, instead of being played with, perhaps Saul would not have had to listen to his enemy humiliate and curse him for forty days, morning and afternoon.

The Curse of Goliath: Spectating instead of participating

I believe the curses Goliath placed on God's army were fear of fighting, and to be a spectator and not a participator in the war. The devil uses this same curse on the church today. But guess what? GOD WANTS AN ARMY – NOT AN AUDIENCE!! I will say this again: *Christianity is not a spectator sport!* Today we have to break this curse of spectating and being an audience off of God's army in Jesus' name. We need to step out and take proactive measures in our life to counteract our weaknesses and protect ourselves as fellow soldiers in God's army.

The Word says, *"Be doers of the word, and not hearers only, deceiving yourselves."* (James 1: 22) In a practical sense, that means "Don't just be a spectator. Be a participator as well."

Have you ever worked on a crew in a kitchen, in construction, or on a special project at school or at work? In those circumstances, everyone must work together and at least bear their own load. What do you think about a lazy team member who stands around and watches everyone else do the work? How much more does it affect the Kingdom of God? What do people think when they consider your work efforts in the Body of Christ? What do you want them to think? What will you do about it?

Can't you get that stupid dog to stop barking?

What thoughts were going through Saul's mind during the forty days he heard the bellowing of Goliath morning and afternoon? How could he stand to hear the humiliating accusations and curses from his enemy in front of everybody for so long?

Goliath was following the example of his father the devil, as satan is the *"accuser of our brethren."* (Revelations 12: 10) Thank God for Jesus our victorious advocate before the Father! (I John 2: 1)

Waiting till the dog loses it's voice is no way to get it to stop barking. You have to face it and shut it up yourself.

I look good, but I don't feel good
While he listened to the barking of Goliath twice daily for those forty long, embarrassing, hopeless days, Saul looked the impressive role of a king. He was surrounded by his entourage, and he was doing a good job of showing up and appearing strong.

Appearances are not always reality. Living your life worrying about the opinions of others or what they think of you is a weak and empty way to go through life. Do you appear to be a good Christian, but are slipping in secret areas no one knows about? Does it look like you have your life in order, when inside things are really falling apart? Do you have Goliaths in your life from whom you have endured continual barking but you have been unable to conquer?

Despite his appearance as a strong king, Saul could not affect victory in his life because he refused to obey God, humble himself, and turn from his sin. I am sure Saul was desperate for God to move. However, Saul was not desperate enough to move to God.

How about us? We are faced with the same Goliaths day after day, year after year. We can hear sermon after sermon, yet still go home the same troubled people. I think one of the dumbest things a person can do is to have the power to change a bad situation but not do it. For instance, starving to death when seated at a sumptuous feast while the food gets cold would be nothing short of an idiotic waste.

Our spirits are starving and we run to and fro looking to be blessed and fed, yet we ignore the feast of God's Word always laid before us. You cannot eat until you determine to pick up the fork! You read your Bible, but are you seeking direction or are you reading from obligation? You pray, but are you learning to get close to God in worship and friendship, or does it seem like you are "going through the motions?"

As Saul can now tell you, there is a lot more to the fight than just showing up and looking good. You cannot have power from God by only going through the motions. Going to church is wonderful, but it is not all of the answer.

Anointing is great, but what about the power and character to persevere? Are you spending time with God in prayer? Are you getting more than a daily verse once or twice a week for your Bible study time? Are you asking for the spiritual authority and strength to conquer the problems in your life? Do you have a relationship with God that causes you to willing crucify your flesh and walk in the Spirit? Do you love God so much more than your favorite TV program that you will turn off the show to spend time with Him? Do you have, or have you asked God to give you, a thirst for righteousness and for winning the lost?

You can take the steps right now so that you can conquer the Goliaths in your life. Do not listen to Goliath any longer than it takes you to call on the name of Jesus!

Hey, is there a champion in the house?
Saul's final tragic fault was in looking for a champion, instead of being a champion or training a champion. Saul was all too quick to let someone else risk his or her life, when it should have been him. Perhaps Saul offered his armor to David so that people would think it was him out there fighting Goliath. Nevertheless, God still moved on behalf of His covenants and promises for Israel. God raised up a champion to fight and defeat the enemy.

At least Saul was smart enough to step out of the way and let someone go on the battlefield. He was all too willing to let anybody go fight his battle. Let someone else risk their life and tell me how it turns out. God bless you. Be blessed, be filled, be gone. Unfortunately, Saul let David go onto the battlefield unprotected. Let's be a covering, support, and reinforcement for each other when we have to go out to fight our Goliaths.

But I don't want to train anybody

Too often we do not go on to the fight ourselves when we should. Other times we block new champions from being raised up by not training them, by not allowing them on the battlefield, or by not giving potential champions a battle to fight.

Perhaps if Saul had mentored a soldier into being a warrior there might not have been a need for David to come along. How many ministries or works have you seen die off, or not begin, because a successor or leader was not trained or prepared? How many businesses have suffered because of a lack of a trained successor? David, through his humble faithful service as a shepherd, was trained personally by God Himself for the work of destroying Goliath, and for later being king over God's people.

Why are we reluctant to train warriors and let new champions on the battlefield? Maybe we do not know how to allow them, or know who they are. Perhaps we have issues with delegation. Did you know warriors in training are not only yourself, but also are probably your spouse, your children, your co-workers, your friends, and maybe your neighbors? We all must join the fight to win this war. We all have a greater purpose to perform, but we must be given the chance to fight for it.

Are you waiting to feel "spiritual" before you start training them or yourself? Do not wait till you feel spiritual because by waiting instead of preparing, you will never "feel spiritual." You will just have to keep watching and listening to your Goliaths bellow profanities and curses at you.

Often we do not train others because we are too selfish to allow someone else to share the limelight in God's work. What if our protégé is better than we are? Also, it is frustrating and time consuming training a new warrior. This inexperienced person often may be immature in things and skills important to you.

Maybe we do not raise up new champions because we are afraid they may really screw things up. Maybe they might embarrass us, or they will not do the work as well as us.

Finally, and most importantly, many people need a ministry, or at least something meaningful to do, to maintain their interest and faithfulness in church and God's training process. Without training warriors and giving them skirmishes, we weaken the army of God. We can block the hand of God from moving and helping by not properly training and equipping the army of God.

You train champions by spending meaningful time with them. Learn the strengths and weaknesses of the potential candidate. Reinforce the weak areas, but teach your champion candidates to focus on and use their strengths. To the best of your ability encourage those in your sphere of influence to take opportunities that will stretch and challenge their capabilities.

How much authority do you give them in these training exercises? Give them enough authority and control to make their own mistakes. It's not all about "sink or swim" either. They may need a little help in the water until they learn how to swim. Help them when they need it, but don't drown them in expectations and pressure. Ask the Lord to help you train new champions. For more on this topic I highly recommend any material by Dr. John C. Maxwell. You can find his material at www.injoy.com.

God's champions are not Russian dolls

I remember reading an article from *The Wall Street Journal* some years ago when the Journal interviewed David Ogilvy, the self made millionaire advertising executive and founder of the wildly successful Madison Avenue advertising agency Ogilvy & Mather. Ogilvy in his interview stated that at a difficult and critical period in his company's history, he had a meeting of his managers and directors where he gave everyone in the room a Russian doll.

This doll would open and there would be a smaller doll inside. Then the next smaller doll would open to reveal an even smaller doll, and so on, until the final doll opened to reveal a message. The message was "If we continue to hire people with lesser abilities than ourselves, we will quickly become a company of dwarves."

Do not be intimidated if someone you are training has more talents or promise than you. Rejoice because you have helped raise up a warrior and champion that you may need to call on to rescue you someday.

By helping to train them you can share in that person's future fruit, so why not make sure that you help them so your future rewards are greater. You are investing in your future. Remember we are all soldiers in the same army.

Friendly fire?
Let's not cause casualties with "friendly fire." Friendly fire is when the army's artillery hits some of its own instead of hitting the enemy. This tragedy happens when we fail to distinguish the enemy from our own forces.

We only have one enemy. Our enemy is not anybody or anything that gets in our way, that is different than us, or is not nice to us. Our only enemy is satan and his kingdom. Our enemy is not unbelievers. Think of them as slaves or prisoners of war that we are fighting to help free. Our enemy is the sin that is in the world that brings people into bondage, not those that are bound, even if they don't agree with us. Our enemy is certainly not one another and clearly not different churches or different denominations.

During a period as a Christian, I lived a hypocritical life that included bar hopping and promiscuous sexual activity while I was faithfully attending a good church. Unfortunately what I found for a while was that people at the clubs and bars were nicer to me than my Christian brothers and sisters I had at church.

It is unfortunate that our deepest wounds and offenses can come at the hands of God's people. Don't get me wrong. I am not blaming them for my mistakes, which I take full credit for. No one was forcing me to run around like I did. Fortunately I discovered later that the world's friendliness was a cheap counterfeit masking hidden bondage, emptiness, and death. What a shame when drunks can be nicer than born again believers!

Let's get a focus for who we are really fighting and how we can help each other do the work and win the battles that we all face.

But I need, I need.
Every church in the world has a need for more workers, more laborers in the Harvest. There are always things that can be done. There certainly was a need for someone to conquer Goliath.

Need alone is an improper motivation for trying to be a champion. It was a good thing that David was anointed/empowered to be the champion of Goliath. The results could have been disastrous both for David and the army of Israel if David had been trying to address a need he was not called to.

II Corinthians 9: 7 tells us how to give and how to do God's work. *"So let each one give as he purposes in his heart, not grudgingly or of necessity; for God loves a cheerful giver."* Do not be motivated by need. Be led by God.

There is always a need for more: more money, more time, more work, more help. If your work, giving, or ministering are based on need alone, instead of as God purposes in your heart, you will never be able to enjoy life or your accomplishments. Why? Because you will never be able to bring anything to completion. There will always be something else that needs to be done. You will be in danger of being burned out by running from need to need.

For more on this topic, and on how to effectively receive more from God, look for my upcoming book called *Reaping, Sowing and Flowing.*

You can pick your friends,..., but do you know how to pick your fights?
How do you know which fights to be in? In other words, how do I know the area I should work in or where I should try to help fill a need?

First, you prepare and train for the battle by developing and maintaining a consistent fellowship with God in prayer, praise, and His word. Seek His will and ask God to lead you in it. Then use the skills God has given you and walk through the doors He has opened.

Realize that every opportunity before you is not always a door God has opened. Sometimes satan will send a counterfeit to distract or disarm you. T.D. Jakes said it best when he said, "I used to thank God for the doors He opened. Now I thank God for the doors He closed."

You can rest in the scripture David penned that, *"The steps of a good man are ordered by the Lord."* (Psalms 37: 23a)

Do not be upset if the Lord has closed a door. That usually signifies a battle you were not meant to fight, and it means you are one door closer to the one you are supposed to walk through.

Chapter 12

Preparing to Face Your Enemy

Now Eliab his oldest brother heard when he spoke to the men; and Eliab's anger was aroused against David, and he said, "Why did you come down here? And with whom have you left those few sheep in the wilderness? I know your pride and the insolence of your heart, for you have come down to see the battle." And David said, "What have I done now? Is there not a cause?" Then he turned from him toward another and said the same thing; and these people answered him as the first ones did. (I Samuel 17: 28 – 30)

He ain't heavy – He's my brother
Even before he had the chance to meet Saul, someone close to David was already trying to demean and demotivate him. With David's brother's comments we recognize that often when you try to do something good or share your vision, there is someone close to you trying to pull you down or who thinks that your confidence is pride. How should you deal with it? Do what David did – ignore them, do not even give them a response. Go forward in what God has ordained you to do.

Does it hurt to leave behind those you love? Yes, but remember Jesus' words, "*...there is no one who has left house or brothers or sisters or father or mother or wife or children or lands, for My sake and the gospel's, who shall not receive a hundredfold now in this time...and in the age to come, eternal life.*" (Mark 10: 29, 30).

Not everyone, even your spiritual or biological brothers and sisters, will be supportive or approving of your vision or your gifts. Maybe that is why Jesus said to not cast your pearls before swine. (Matthew 7:6) Not to imply that people that do not agree with you are swine, but rather, this teaching instructs us to not waste your most precious things with someone who will not appreciate or use them.

David served God and his direction came from his Master. As long as you have been sent by God, and not of your own accord, do not let the questions or disapproval of others stop you from doing what you need to do to fulfill your God-given visions and dreams. Don't be another Jonathan who resented the lack of approval from others which caused him to never do anything great again.

We know our God is a jealous God (Exodus 20: 5). A jealous God does not want anybody other than Himself playing the role of Master in your life. Do you think God is pleased when you take orders or suggestions from sources other than Him? If you are employed at McDonald's, can the Burger King manager come in to your store and demand that you unload her truck?

Public opinion vs. Spiritual counsel

Many times people will have God-given gifts, dreams, or visions, but they step out to face their Goliath too soon. Sometimes they have been warned by pastors and friends that they were not ready. Instead of heeding good counsel, they mistake the spiritual advisors as "swine" before whom their pearls should not have been cast. Ignoring counsel, the one with the vision and dream will step out. Upon failing, he or she will blame God for the defeat. When all the while, although they may have had their own AC/PC, they were not operating in the timing and blessing of their Master, so they fought on their own strength and failed.

It is important to listen to the advice of your spiritual advisors when it comes to stepping out and implementing your vision and dreams. The Bible says there is safety in much counsel. (Proverbs 11: 14)

How are you to receive counsel? First, listen to the wise counsel of the godly. Next, take the counsel to God in prayer. Wait to act until you get an answer from God. If you don't get an answer from God, step back and look at the situation.

Never be pushed or manipulated into doing anything. Remember God's nature is to lead and that satan's nature is to push and manipulate. If you feel you are being pushed, it is almost always the devil. If you feel like you are being led, it is almost always God.

Once you have determined the correct course based on God's leading, act on the answer at the proper time.

Listening and heeding good counsel could have saved many people the pain and depression of wounds from lost battles. The cause was right and they were the right people to fight the battle, but the timing was wrong. Unfortunately, like Jonathan many of these well meaning people will never try to step out again, even when the timing is right. This is another practical example of the scripture *"Many are called, but few are chosen."*

Well, I have to tell SOMEBODY
We all like good news. We all like good things. Often we want to share them with others. Especially if it is as significant as our gifts, vision and purpose. How should we share them with others?

When told by the angel that she would give birth to Jesus, Mary gave us the best example of how to deal with expressing your gifts, vision, and purpose. It says in Luke 1 after the great spiritual experience with the angel that *"Mary pondered those things in her heart."*

I am sure that eventually Mary was forced to share the angelic occurrence, particularly when the signs of her immaculate conception started to show! But she did not tell that account to everyone, not even the people who were undoubtedly spreading vile rumors about her.

Mary did not become "overly spiritual" about the angelic visitation. Sometimes people experience a great or powerful spiritual encounter that, if taken in an improper way, may cause some to overemphasize spiritual matters. As my mother was so fond of reminding me when I first became a Christian, "even Christ had to walk the earth, so you should too." She used to tell me that new born-again Christians should be locked up for a year or two with each other until they could learn to walk on the ground again!

An overemphasis on spiritual occurrences will disable or consume you from your earthly everyday functions necessary for God to manifest His spiritual purposes, your AC/PC. The visit from the angel did not disable or consume Mary. The angelic visit was great, but she was going to be a mother. The practical implications of her AC/PC far outweighed the emotionalism of the spiritual encounter.

There is a right time, a right way, and right people with whom to share your vision, anointing, gifts, and purpose. Remember, you do not have to tell everyone your goals and your dreams. You do not have to prove to anybody that God has gifted or anointed you. Do not be ashamed of anything the Lord has blessed you with. Rather be wise in when, how, and with whom you are talking about them.

Before you share your vision, your anointing, gifts, or purpose with anyone, you need to question your motive for revealing these things. Is it to bless someone or are you trying to attract friends, approval, or an audience? Are you sharing these things to contact someone who can bring you closer to the King, or are there underlying motives based in pride? When you do share these things, do not let negative comments keep you from doing what you know you need to do, when it is the right time.

David did not look for his brother's approval or ask permission to fight Goliath. I am sure David's brother did not say those same negative things to David when he walked back with Goliath's head in his hand! Remember, you serve God, and God is the only One you have to prove anything to regardless of what anybody says, does, or thinks.

You also have to be careful not to share your vision with spiritually immature people, like David's brother, who might try to dissuade you from trying to fulfill your dreams. David's brother tried to use manipulation and accusations to keep David from changing the atmosphere and defeating Goliath. Satan still uses those same tactics against us to keep us from attacking our problems. Do not be stopped by someone else's vision (or lack thereof) for you!

You can never find a good tailor when you need one
So Saul clothed David with his armor, and he put a bronze helmet on his head; he also clothed him with a coat of mail. David fastened his sword to his armor and tried to walk, for he had not tested them. And

David said to Saul, "I cannot walk with these, for I have not tested them." So David took them off. (I Samuel 17: 38, 39)

When David was offered Saul's armor he refused to wear it. He said he had not proved them. He was not worthy of them, or familiar with them, because he did not have any experience with Saul's adornments. David could not even walk while wearing Saul's armor! David could not be something he was not. He had to be real and honest in order to survive the fight he was facing. His life depended on it.

David did not fall for the trap of people's well-meaning suggestions. Sometimes even the best or most logical suggestions can cause you to veer from your focus or your strengths. David could not try to be Saul and win. He had to be himself.

You cannot fight the fight for God by trying to be like anybody else other than Jesus and the person He has made you to be. You must walk in those talents and abilities God has given you. Instead of trying to be something he was not, David chose to use a seemingly insignificant skill he was an expert in – the sling. Talk about "showing up at a gunfight with a knife."

To the spectators it looked like the odds were impossible. The message is this: If God truly called you, with the proper preparation and timing you are good enough for Him, and you are good enough for anything He places you in. Just know and be you. Be careful to guard yourself so you stay focused in the right direction.

The smooth stone Maker
Then he took his staff in his hand; and he chose for himself five smooth stones from the brook, and put them in a shepherd's bag, in a pouch which he had, and his sling was in his hand. (I Samuel 17: 40)

Have you ever considered that God intentionally created an impossible situation? God ordered the use of an unlikely weapon, a shepherd's sling. This was done so that David could operate from his strength and advantage and so that God could get the glory for performing a miracle. When God calls you, He will use what you have or He will give you something else to work with.

Focusing on our strengths will give us far greater success than focusing on improving our weaknesses. We all have weaknesses, and they cannot be ignored. But when you enter life's battlefield, we must give ourselves as much advantage as possible. That only comes from focusing on and enhancing our strengths. We do not need someone else's strength; we need to use the strengths we have. No matter how insignificant or unconventional.

Remember when Gideon was visited by God, and he was called/anointed to lead the Israelites to victory? God told Gideon to "*Go in this thy might.*" (Judges 6: 14 KJV) Perhaps this could mean to "go in the strength that you have." Gideon was not told to get someone else's strength, or even try to be anyone else. If God had wanted anyone or anything else, believe me friend, He would have gotten it!

Unconventional weapons hit the enemy with something he does not expect. You cannot defeat the enemy on his turf, his terms, or with his weapons. Exchange the natural weapons of your mouth, your ability, and your posturing with spiritual weapons – the FIVE SMOOTH STONES.

What does he know that I don't know?
Have you ever wondered why God uses small things to fight big things? It is because God has already fought and won the battle before we show up. All God needs is someone to go in and manifest and posses the work He has already done.

God does not fight the enemy on the enemy's terms or turf. The enemy may have a great champion or impressive armies, but God has already won the battle. So the Lord can send in a kid with some rocks to defeat the meanest and toughest champion.

When God uses the young and tiny to defeat the great and mighty that really proves God is in control. Do you want to know what the devil knows that he doesn't want you to know. The devil has already been totally defeated. All he can do now is to try to delay the time from you realizing that he has already lost.

The next time the devil tries to depress or demotivate you, remind him that you are a child of God and that Jesus has already conquered him. As such, all you have to do is show up, stand your ground, be obedient, stay settled in God's process, continue to seek, and let the Lord win your battle for you. You may have to get on the battlefield and throw the stone, *i.e.* take steps to activate God's plan, but realize that if you are in God's will you are never outnumbered.

Get FIVE to stay alive!

Why did David take five stones? Was the shepherd that unsure about his aim? Did you know the Bible teaches us that Goliath had four sons who were also giants? (II Samuel 21:18-22) David wanted enough ammunition to eliminate all of his enemies.

David purposed in his heart as he walked into that valley that when he was done, his enemy would be dead. He would not accept the enemy's battle terms because he knew Who and Whose he was and what his authority and abilities were through his AC/PC power.

We pray for deliverance from problems, curses, evil habits, and sin, yet we walk back into those same things that put us in bondage in the first place. Did David try to sew Goliath's head back on after he cut it off? If you want to live free and not have to serve the enemy, then face your Goliaths, conquer them through Jesus' name, and let them stay dead in the valley. Then you can grab your enemy's decapitated head and show it to the people that tried to discourage you from reaching your goals or show your enemy's head to the next guy who tries to attack you.

The total purpose of the fivefold ministries

The five stones of David symbolize critically important weapons in our spiritual arsenal today: the "fivefold ministries" as talked about in Ephesians chapter 4. In his previously mentioned "Prophets" series of Books and in his books *The Eternal Church* and *Apostles, Prophets and the Coming Moves of God*, Dr. Bill Hamon outlines a Biblical foundation for the restoration of all the fivefold ministries, and the necessity of this total restoration prior to Jesus' return.

Without reciting his excellent works or writing a book on the subject myself, I cannot truly communicate the total significance of the fivefold ministries and their role in God's end-time plans for planet earth. Needless to say, the individual components of the fivefold ministries, whether one or all, are the lifeblood of any movement of God in modern times. We need to learn how to daily and practically incorporate the work of the fivefold ministries into our spiritual warfare and earthly works as leaders, followers, and fellow laborers.

And He Himself gave some to be apostles, some prophets, some evangelists, and some pastors and teachers, for the equipping of the saints for the work of ministry, for the edifying of the body of Christ, till we all come to the unity of the faith and of the knowledge of the Son of God, to a perfect man, to the measure of the stature of the fullness of Christ... (Ephesians 4: 11-13)

These ministries were given for the equipping of the saints to make us strong enough to conquer the Goliaths in our lives. You have five fingers on your hand and the fivefold ministries, through us, are the hand of God on earth. Did you know that most jewels are just highly polished smooth stones? The fivefold ministries are like David's five smooth stones. They are our weapons and our jewels. They are precious and should be utilized and protected.

Become a "smoothie"

Why did they have to be smooth stones? A jagged stone or a stone that was broken was actually unstable and could not ever fly straight enough to complete the task of hitting a target aimed at. And you thought your frustration for everything always going wrong was bad luck or the devil's attacks. If you are jagged this may have been caused by inconsistent spiritual habits; or being offended or offensive, harsh, critical, or selfish. Unfortunately if you are jagged you will not "fly straight" and you will find it increasingly difficult to ever obtain your goals with any satisfaction.

Jagged stones are not caused by bad luck or even the devil. They are caused by the stone not being in the polishing place long enough to become smooth and effective. They are also caused by the consequences of bad choices made throughout life. It is because your stone is jagged that it cannot fly straight enough to follow through and successfully reach its target. That is why it is critically important for us to walk in spiritual maturity and stability.

It takes maturity to be smooth and to "fly straight." David had to reach to the bottom of the brook to get the really smooth stones. They were the ones that sat under the surface, that were behind the scenes or had been seemingly forgotten by others.

Being on the bottom of life for a while will smooth your stone if you let it. I've got good news for you. If you're at rock bottom, it's not over yet! You're finally at the place where God can use you!

Being at rock bottom God can use you if you let Him pick you up and put you in His sling. Hallelujah! Those stones David grabbed were solid and had been made smooth by being at the bottom of the brook and staying in the smoothing process long enough for the water to naturally make them smooth. Do not complain about being at or coming from the bottom of the brook. The bottom of the brook can make you smooth and polished if you remain obedient in the process.

People like to look at, touch, and play with smooth stones like jewelry or marbles. Jagged and sharp stones are always left alone unless they're used to harm someone else. As Christians we have to be mature, stable: a polished stone. The process to make us that way sometimes requires that we stay at the bottom of the brook for a while, often longer than we want. Do not waste time waiting though. Use your tenure at brook's bottom to get smooth and to take the steps to prepare, perfect, and mature yourself.

Our Lord and Savior Himself prepared thirty years for a ministry that only lasted three. Like the stone at the bottom of the brook, stay settled in God's process of growth towards maturity, stability, and spiritual refinement. If you do not strive for or stay in His process, then you will never be smooth enough to ever hit the mark, and you will easily breed distraction, discouragement, and offense in yourself and others.

Does the little thing I do matter?

You may never know if that little job or task you do, the help you give someone, or the prayers you pray, are not the smooth stone, or weapon, needed at that time to knock down someone's Goliath. Remember, David was fighting somebody else's battle (God's and Saul's), not his own. Sometimes you may never realize the impact of the small things you do without ever getting glory or recognition. Remember, the Word says *"What is done secretly God will reward openly."* (Matthew 6: 4) So, *"Be not weary in well doing."* (Galatians 6: 9)

The stones David grabbed were small and were concealed from sight until they were used. David was able to "fly under the radar." That phrase means he was able to attack his enemy without being detected or attacked himself. God often uses this tactic to destroy his enemies. If David had been playing with the stones out in the open he could have misplaced or dropped his weapons. If David was a high profile figure, then the enemy would have been better prepared to face him. Maybe if Goliath had seen the weapon in advance of David using it against him, he may have realized his vulnerability and covered his forehead before David slung the stone. By "flying under the radar" David was able to surprise his enemy. There are advantages to avoiding a high profile.

Make the stones you throw, your testimony and the work of your hands and your mind, smooth and excellent in God's sight, protected and concealed until you need them. Don't parade your strengths in front of anyone. That way your ammunition will always be ready to surprise your enemy and you can hit your target. In so doing you will glorify and please your Maker all while not being an attack from the enemy.

The Gemologist and the stone

If you think you may have jagged stones in your life, repent and submit yourself to the Master Gemologist for finishing. Remember what it says in Hebrews 12: 2 – Jesus is the author and finisher of our faith. Let the Lord polish (finish) the jagged areas of your life.

How do rough stones become precious? The gemologist takes a rough stone, ugly in everybody else's opinion, and spends time with it, cleaning and preparing it to transform it into a precious gem. The gemologist takes his tools and hour upon hour polishes the stone so that someday it will fit into a setting for jewelry.

Do you ever wonder what the gem, if it had an opinion and could talk, would say during the polishing process? The stone would probably complain that the process hurt and that it took too long! Of course that rough rock has no comprehension of the beauty it will have as a finished jewel.

God works with us in much the same way. He is trying to polish us into being a smooth stone, one that can be used as a jewel in His crown or as a weapon against our enemies.

Inside everyone else's ugly rock the gemologist sees the beautiful gem waiting to be revealed. Inside a life of mistakes, sin, problems, and pain, God sees a wonderful purpose in you that He wants to release and perfect.

To make smooth and polished stones the gemologists repeatedly remove layer after layer of what is on the outside of the stone, the jagged outer crust, until it reaches a consistent surface. The gemologist removes all of the inconsistencies until a uniform and consistent base is formed.

In the same way God tries to remove the inconsistencies in our life to make us spiritually mature and a precious stone in His sight. Submit to God your true self, and let the beauty inside you be made manifest by the Great Creator. Do not build up a hard shell on the outside of religiousness, pride, sinful habits, doubt, worry, depression, fear, or approval seeking that He has to break through and grind off.

Instead, trust Him to make you a vessel of honor and a true jewel in His crown. Let Him take you through the polishing and finishing process by developing consistent godly habits of prayer, praise, Bible study and continuous obedience to God.

*Coming to Him as to a living stone, rejected indeed by men, but chosen by God and **precious** (emphasis added), you also, as living stones, are being built up a spiritual house, a holy priesthood, to offer up spiritual sacrifices acceptable to God through Jesus Christ.* (I Peter 2: 4, 5)

We complain to the Master Gemologist that His polishings hurt and take too long to make us smooth or precious. We think we can jump off of His workbench before we are finished and try to fit into a setting someplace ourselves. Or worse yet, we fling ourselves at our Goliaths and wonder why we are not knocking them down. It is at that point we start to feel like we do not "fit" anywhere, and we complain to the Master Gemologist when it was ourselves that blocked His process for maturity and excellence in our lives.

I just don't seem to fit in

Let's go back to Ephesians 4 and look in verses 15 and 16 for the end result of the work of the fivefold ministries in our lives.

*[B]ut, speaking the truth in love, may grow up in all things into Him who is the head - Christ - from whom the whole body, **fitly* joined together** by what every joint supplies, according to the effective working by which every part does its share, causes growth of the body for the edifying of itself in love.*

**Author's prerogative was used with the quotation of this verse, as Author combined the NKJV text with the KJV word "fitly" to present this verse. Emphasis added.*

Have you ever felt out of place? Maybe you were not "fitly joined together" with where you were at the time. Have you ever tried to force a jigsaw puzzle piece into a place it did not go? Now you understand idea of what I am saying.

Submit to the Master Gemologist for finishing, polishing, and smoothing so you will "fit" in the setting He wants you to be in. Look closely at this scripture. Jesus will use "what every joint supplies" (*i.e.*- other people) to make you "fitly joined together." You cannot try the process of "fitting" by yourself.

We all have a place where we belong. Jesus will use some "apostles, some prophets, some evangelists, and some pastors and teachers" to get us where we need to be and to cause the body to grow itself. Sometimes He'll use spouses, friends, neighbors, children, and other believers to help get us where we need to be. Praise God, Jesus has everything figured out! We just have to find and submit ourselves to what He has already done.

When you get into the right place and get to work, take a look at what happens. Being in the right place and doing what we are supposed to do *"causes growth of the body for the edifying of itself in love."* (Ephesians 4:16b)

When we all get to where we belong and get to do our work effectively, what happens? The body of Christ – the Church – grows itself. Do you want to win the lost, take your city for God, and have a powerful ministry? Do you want a successful business, good career, or a good marriage? Get where you "fit," start doing your work effectively, and let the body "grow itself."

We don't have to fight and struggle to achieve church growth or successful ministries. We just need to get out of the way, go to where we fit, and do our work as effectively as we can. When we do this, God will perform His word by causing the body to "grow itself."

Chapter 13

How To Disarm And Destroy Your Enemy With His Own Weapon

Let's Get Ready To Rumble!
Now, let's catch up to David. By this time he is walking down the hill being watched by his brothers, his king, his countrymen, and enemies he never knew he had. He has taken all the steps he could to prepare for the fight.

David showed up knowing his purpose, his AC/PC, and his limitations. He was totally submitted to God, walking in relationship with Him, and willing to do whatever He wanted. David knew the encounters with the lion and the bear were used to train him for this day. He knew he could not wear the king's armor and be something he was not. David knew that he could only give the battle to God and use his God-given expertise and strengths to defeat Goliath.

Most importantly, David knew that a death was going to occur in that valley. He knew that both he and Goliath were not going to walk out alive. David knew and trusted God, so much that he was willing to give his life for the Lord's purpose.

For God to eliminate your enemies (your obstacles), you have to be willing to "die" for the Lord. You do this by being willing to give your life for whatever He wants you to do in the battles that He sends you into.

We know how David manifested victory in the physical realm. He threw the stone and then cut off Goliath's head. But let's shift our focus to how David manifested victory in the spiritual realm.

David was sent by God to fight Goliath. God had enough faith in David's abilities to obey and trust Him that He sent him to face this enemy. Do not complain or be overwhelmed by the obstacles and enemies you face, even if they are nine feet tall like Goliath. If the Lord sends you into battle, it means that He trusts you with that situation. Learn to distinguish between the battles that are distractions and the battles that were sent from God for you to fight.

There were probably a lot of evil people bellowing profanities and curses at that time, but David did not have to fight any of them except Goliath. Facing any of the other Philistines would have been a distraction from his true purpose, an utter waste of time, and probably an unnecessary risk.

If you choose a fight, make sure it is one God has sent you to. If you are facing an enemy, remember it was God who sent you just like He sent David. Be convinced of this: you can face the obstacle before you now and win!

David realized Goliath was fighting against God, not David. Remember the scripture in Ephesians 6: 12, 13: *"For we do not wrestle against flesh and blood, but against principalities, against powers, against the rulers of the darkness of this age, against spiritual hosts of wickedness in the heavenly places. Therefore take up the whole armor of God, that you may be able to withstand in the evil day, and having done all, to stand."*

David set up God to get glory. He faced his fears and he turned the battle over to God. How did he do it? He did it by what he believed in his heart, by what he proclaimed to his adversary, and by his actual actions.

If we have already won, why do I have to fight?
"This day the LORD will deliver you into my hand, and I will strike you and take your head from you. And this day I will give the carcasses of the camp of the Philistines to the birds of the air and the wild beasts of the earth, that all the earth may know that there is a God in Israel. Then all this assembly shall know that the LORD does not save with sword and spear; ***for the battle is the Lord's, and He will give you into our hands."*** *(Emphasis added)* (I Sam. 17: 46,47)

Please note that David still had to throw the stone, even though it was God's battle. David still had to have the vision of the work being accomplished before he knew where to aim that lethal stone. We get upset sometimes at battles we lose, when we never gave the battle to God to fight to begin with, or we never had a focused enough vision for the stone to hit its mark.

Sometimes people fight battles and do not know why. We struggle and struggle, but what is the reason? Have you ever heard of a Pyrrhic victory? That is a victory, that if you win, the cost of it was not worth what you gained. Arguing with people, proving points, expensive legal battles, divorces, dissolution of partnerships, church splits, and other emotionally costly conflicts can sometimes be considered Pyrrhic victories. I am not advocating that you avoid conflict, as I believe that we could eliminate many problems if we had the strength and character to deal directly and promptly with issues. David did not run from Goliath, he marched right down to meet Goliath and end his evil influence once and for all.

I feel strongly though that we must prayerfully consider the conflicts or fights we engage in, and know before we start that the victory is worth the cost of battle. In David's conflict with Goliath, the freedom of the nation of Israel and God's reputation to protect His people were the reasons for the conflict. Be certain that the conflict is worth the cost, and that you are actually dealing with the true source of your problems.

Great victories rarely fall out of the sky. YOU still have to walk in the valley, face the enemy, and trust God for a miracle. My friend George still had to take music lessons and practice. Elisha still had to follow hard to get the mantle and double anointing. I still had to study, pray, and type for hundreds of hours for you to read what is on these pages.

Again we see why vision is so critical. If David threw the stone in the wrong place, then Goliath would have struck and killed David while he was reloading the sling or while he was looking the wrong way. We blame God for getting blindsided by the enemy sometimes, when in fact the enemy's unseen attack was enabled by us looking in the wrong place.

What is one way we can have misplaced vision? When our intention was to fight the battle our way, get glory for ourselves, or not to give it God. Walking into the valley to fight too early or too late can also be misplaced vision. The most obvious cause of misplaced vision is to not have clearly defined goals. This is why written plans, mission statements, and clearly defined goals are critical for success. You have to know that target you are aiming for!

> *Write the vision and make it plain on tablets,*
> *that he may run who reads it* (Habakkuk 2: 2)

We all intimately know the problems that grow from picking a fight we don't belong in. Why then do we try to fight battles we were not called to, did not have faith in God for, or that we never gave to God?

What about if we are using the wrong weapons? What if we are looking for someone else to fight instead of fighting ourselves? And what happens if we did not proclaim a coming victory to our enemies or our actions never followed through with victorious living?

Failing to take all of these steps does not guarantee failure, it just means that we lessen our chance of consistently hitting our mark. A jagged stone might have been able to knock down Goliath, but the stakes of the battle were too high to proceed in uncertainty. It is when we fail in knocking down Goliath that we get upset, frustrated, and doubtful. We feel that the Lord is not helping us enough. But how can we blame God for the "Goliaths" we worked to create? Why does God not remove these obstacles that seem to always be in front of us?

God had the power and authority to send an angelic host at any time to kill Goliath and wipe out the Philistines. So why didn't He? God gives us skirmishes to face so that He can train and raise up the champion within us. But when we face adversaries, we cower away from the fight instead of facing it. Thereby we miss an opportunity to become a stronger and better trained champion for Jesus. Have you prayed for God to make you spiritually stronger? Then get ready for the skirmishes!

Rather than readying ourselves for skirmishes, we pray and give God our problems, thinking the Lord will send some mystical force to fix all wrongs while we sleep. David still had to walk down into the valley in front of his adversary, know and focus his vision, follow through by throwing the stone, and decapitate Goliath with his own two hands.

Unless God intervenes supernaturally, He expects us to go and execute His battle with the time, strength, knowledge, skills, and weapons He gave us. We still have to fight because we are the Body of Christ. The Body is what does the work for God in this physical world.

What is the most powerful weapon the Father gave us? It's His Word. David believed and spoke the Word of God and it was his weapon! David relied on the promises of God from scripture and his AC/PC power to strengthen him to know that he could conquer the enemy. I wonder if David "felt" like a champion when he was walking down the hill toward Goliath? I wonder if his feelings that day really mattered?

Feelings, nothing more than feelings, WOE! WOE! WOE! Feelings!

Do you know who you are in Christ Jesus? Did you know He called you to be more than a conqueror through Him that loved you, no matter how jagged your "stone" may be now? (Romans 8: 37) This purpose and calling you have is not dependent on whether or not you feel like a conqueror or if you feel victorious.

David knew from his AC/PC that he was ordained by God to conquer his enemies. David trusted what God said so much that he grabbed his sling and his pouch and put his life on the line to face Goliath. David developed a faith in God that was not based on his feelings. Believe me, I doubt if David "felt" like facing Goliath that or any other day.

Your enemy does not care about your feelings. Your only enemy, the devil and his kingdom, is very glad that you rely on your feelings so much. The devil does not want you to use your real weapons: God's Word, your faith, and the strength, knowledge, and spiritual skills Jesus gave you.

David's enemies were the enemies of God's people, that opposition that seeks to enslave you and the rest of the army of God. Who do you think are your enemies? What is your motivation for being opposed to them?

Mommy – that kid's being mean to me!
Your enemy, satan, hates you and wants you dead and destroyed. Do you remember growing up in your neighborhood? If you were like me, you avoided hanging around people who did not like you or who abused you. You knew that every time you had dealings with that person or that group, you would walk away physically or emotionally hurt.

Why is it different now that we have grown? Why do we keep going back for more punishment and abuse at the hand of the devil? Why do we continue to lust after evil and worldly things, knowing that evil worldly things are at enmity with God? (James 4: 4) You cannot sleep with the enemy and wake up with your life.

We live in this world and we should enjoy the good things of this world. We should unconditionally love the people in this world, regardless of their opinion or what they have done. But we cannot let ourselves be abused or bound by the world. We do not hate the world or the things in it. It is the sin and the cause of the sin (the devil) that we hate and that is our enemy.

So what's the secret ingredient?
The final secret to David's victory in the spiritual realm is that David got a vision of doing and finishing a work: defeating Goliath. His vision was not limited to the target of his attack, but included his victory through God. Because of his vision he was able to properly focus on the target, and he did not stop until he had flung the stone that dropped his enemy at his feet.

Before we ever step into the valley of our Goliaths, we have to get a vision for the battles we are supposed to fight. Then we have to envision ourselves conquering through God. Remember, stay up on the hill and prepare yourself in prayer and the Word until you are ready to use your gifts and strengths to hack off Goliath's head.

How would your face look on a box of Wheaties?
When God created man He placed in him a desire and drive to be a champion. That is why we are so competitive today. Young children grow up wishing to be sports heroes, models, actors, rock stars – the popular champions of our age.

This verse plainly describes how God births in us a desire to be a champion:

*For it is God who works in you both to **will** and to **do** for His good pleasure.* (emphasis added) (Philippians 2: 13)

We dream about conquests and victories, and I believe this dreaming in its right context is natural and from God. We love fantasizing about being a champion and do not even know it. We have natural urges given by God to dream and to succeed, yet when we become sanctified we stifle ourselves by not thinking that God wants us to be successful.

When you are in relationship with Jesus, He will birth in you a "will" (that vision, desire, dream, and drive) to be a champion: for you to "do" something. That is how you get purpose and call. The Lord must birth in you a will for you to do something for His good pleasure.

So many of us have been erroneously taught that God's primary function is to correct and change us to get rid of our sins and mistakes. The concept of God birthing a desire to be a champion is more difficult for us to fathom.

Does God really want me to succeed, or is He always trying to judge me? It took me over twenty years as a Christian to realize that God was on my side and that He wanted me to be successful. During this whole time Jesus was waiting for me to stand up, stop fantasizing about being a champion, and just get down to fighting my Goliath and becoming a champion.

God's success does not guarantee that you will be wealthy, famous, or free from problems or mistakes. But God's plan for your success is for you to live an overcoming, happy, meaningful, peaceful life free of bondage. While fulfilling your God-given purpose, Jesus wants your needs met to the point that you have an abundance of strength and resources to bless others.

For so long we have believed a lie that all God will do is barely meet our needs, at the last minute or just in time. We shy away from thinking that God will actually give us the desires of our hearts or an abundance because to think that is selfish.

Do not ever apologize for the blessings of God, the gifts of God, the anointing of God, or the dream or vision from God to achieve any of those things. Instead, use them to fulfill your God-given dreams and visions.

Where there is no dream – *no vision* – the people perish. (Proverbs 29: 18) They perish because with no vision, there is no champion. With no vision, there is no goal to be attained. With no vision, there is no reason to do anything different. God is looking for champions with a fresh vision. Will you be the one?

David really knew how to get a-head
So it was, when the Philistine arose and came and drew near to meet David, **that David hastened and ran toward the army to meet the Philistine.** *(emphasis added) Then David put his hand in his bag and took out a stone; and he slung it and struck the Philistine in his forehead, so that the stone sank into his forehead, and he fell on his face to the earth. So David prevailed over the Philistine with a sling and a stone, and struck the Philistine and killed him. But there was no sword in the hand of David. Therefore David ran and stood over the Philistine, took his sword and drew it out of its sheath and killed him, and cut off his head with it.* (I Samuel 17: 48-51)

David did not run from the fight. God's Word says he ran to the fight! In the valley a "feeling dependent" faith would have caused David to run from Goliath instead of running to Goliath. David was not just reacting here. He took an offensive position by running to face his enemy. The stone might not have had the impact and momentum needed to knock down Goliath unless David was running to his enemy. Remember that the next time you are tempted to run from a fight.

Stop putting off problems till tomorrow. Don't let your fears keep you from your dreams and your purpose. Face your problems and fears now. Run to your fight. Make sure you are running decisively enough to build momentum to knock your Goliath down on the first try. Do not wait another day to fix what you should have done forty days prior.

When he hit Goliath with the stone, David knocked him down but he still had to finish the work. The stone did not kill Goliath. If it did, why did David have to cut Goliath's head off? Why then did the Bible not say that the stone killed Goliath instead of just knocking him down? Goliath was not dead until David cut his head off.

We take authority over spiritual forces through prayer in the name of Jesus, but we leave it at that and eventually the spiritual attack returns. Why? Because we have not learned the lesson from David. He knocked Goliath down, but he still had to chop off his head! David was not done until he made his enemy totally powerless.

We have spiritual authority in the name of Jesus. But just praying without a changed attitude and different behavior is like throwing the stone, knocking down Goliath, and not cutting off his head. Without totally severing his head you leave power with your enemy. Remember what David intimately knew: your Goliath will eventually get back up and destroy you if you do not kill him and make him totally powerless against you!

How to chop off a head
Remember the scripture *"faith without works is dead"*? (James 2: 20) While writing this book, I asked God to show me what it really meant

to cut off Goliath's head. In the simplest and most direct terms, the Lord showed me that Goliath's head is chopped off when we <u>do</u> the Word of God. That's it. We do not have to do anything else but believe God's Word so fully that we actually <u>do</u> it and to believe it so much that you obey it, follow it, and share it with others.

What about spiritual attacks that keep returning, even after you repeatedly rebuke them in Jesus' name? In spiritual attacks the enemy usually makes "accusations" against us. We know the devil is the accuser of the brethren. (Revelations 12: 10) What accusations does he make? Usually in an effort to keep you as a spectator, he will remind you of past sins, hurt, bondage, or shortcomings.

Sometimes the devil will also use reminiscing about the past to get you to sin as well. The devil does not care how he reminds you of the past. Whether you are more susceptible to reminiscing or condemnation, satan will use whatever he can to attack you where you are weakest. Your enemy will use anything he can to keep you bound and distracted.

This is the time to "stand on" a scripture. James 4: 7 says *"Submit to God. Resist the devil and he will flee from you."* We can all quote it, but how do we get it to work? You know when the devil is tempting you to sin or is attacking you with condemnation. When that happens I like to pray out loud something like this:

> *Jesus, I thank you that you have saved me and received me with all of my sin, which I believe Your blood has cleansed me from. Father, I submit to You, according to Your word, and I ask You to renew my mind and strengthen my spirit so that I am not living or depending on my strength, but I am living and depending on You. I cannot make it on my strength alone. Holy Spirit give me Your grace, strength, anointing and the spiritual authority now to destroy the yoke of what the devil is trying to put on me. I will not accept the attack of the enemy in my life and I resist it. God, according to Your Word, the devil must now flee. And even though I may not feel it now, I praise and thank You in advance because I know You are doing this for me, by Your Word and not by my*

> *feelings. I thank You Precious Lord and Master because I know You hear me and You will do it to prove Your word true.*

The first time you use this strategy, or something like it, it may seem awkward and difficult to believe that it would work. But don't take my word for it, try it for yourself! This is not "mind over matter." It's God's Word. The Word of God will never fail. You have to keep doing these things and trusting God to make them work in your life.

Do you think David cut off Goliath's head in one swoop or did he have to hack it off? The scripture does not specifically say, but I think there was some work to decapitating Goliath. The bigger your enemy, the more work it takes to chop off his head. So do not be discouraged if you have to repeat this procedure several times until it is totally gone.

Be encouraged with this scripture:

I press toward the goal for the prize of the upward call of God in Christ Jesus. (Philippians 3: 14)

Remember, nothing you have to "press towards" ever falls out of the sky on you. At some point there will be some hard work involved.

To make your enemy powerless, you need to remove or avoid the things that cause you to stumble and be distracted from your true purpose. Maybe you need to get rid of the internet if you cannot keep from viewing pornographic sites. At least get a service that blocks out suspect sites and intentionally destroy or forget the password! Get rid of cable TV if you cannot stop watching things that cause you to sin.

Jesus said it was better to lose your eye than your soul (Matthew 18: 9). That does not mean to mutilate yourself. It means to do whatever is necessary to live a victorious life.

To make your enemy powerless you may not have anything physical to "kill" (God forbid), but you may have relationships with people that cause you to compromise your walk with God. There may be a person that tempts you in an area God delivered you from. You need to cut off the relationship with those individuals until such time as you can influence them more with godliness than they influence you with garbage.

Get back to your valley!
Chopping off Goliath's head was not the fulfillment of a specific prophecy, David's AC/PC, or his vision. It was one of many battles in different forms he had to fight to fulfill his AC/PC. After Goliath, David still had a lot of other battles to fight. He could not rest on old victories, old testimonies, or old glories. He had to thank God for the victory and move on to the next valley.

What then was David's next valley? The valley containing his sheep was the one he would have gone back to had Saul not drafted David to serve him. Later, David had to return to the valleys as a refuge while Saul was chasing him for his life.

When you defeat your Goliath, do not let your ego or fantasies about being a champion keep you from going back to your valley and your sheep – your God-given responsibility. Stay in your "valley" until Jesus brings you into something else. After Goliath, even though he had AC/PC for it, David was not yet ready to sit on the throne of Israel.

In the absence of other more specific direction, after triumph always go back to what you were doing until the Lord opens the next door or you get the call from your King to come play at the palace.

My sword, my sword, my kingdom for a sword!
What did David use to kill Goliath since he brought no sword with his stones and sling? He used Goliath's own sword. What the enemy tries to destroy you with, God will always use as a weapon against him! What the enemy means for evil, God will always use for good. That is how you can turn your weaknesses into strengths.

That sounds good, but how do you use the evil attacks in your life, the weapons coming against you, and your past failures to defeat your adversary? I believe there are at least three ways. They are:

- remembering the impact of past attacks/temptations/failures to motivate you to avoid repeating them
- utilizing past successful strategies against current attacks
- learning to use your attacks as occasions to fall more in love with God.

First of all, if you could get an understanding of what the enemy wants to do to you and keep from you, you would vehemently fight and resist whatever the devil sends. Remember John 10: 10 KJV says, *"The thief cometh not, but for to kill, and to steal, and to destroy."* You may have fun indulging in that sin or habit for a while, but it will ultimately bring you into bondage.

Remembering the hurt, pain, and consequences of past failures diminishes the sweetness and lure of sin. You know every time you deal with that bully he is going to try to hurt you and make you feel bad. So why not always stay as far away from it as possible, instead of trying to see how close to the line you can sneak without getting caught?

Secondly, once you start to achieve victories, you learn how to win. You can build on and remember those strategies that brought you into victory. You see, it is OK to be successful. In essence, you need to learn from your successes at least as much as from your failures. You plainly recognize when you are being spiritually attacked, and no one has to remind you what it is like to lose.

So why not recognize the battle and chose to win instead of repeating a defeat? By keeping a focus on doing what brought you your past success, you can translate proven winning strategies into weapons against whatever is attacking or tempting you now. Does it sound complicated? Usually it is as easy as saying "no."

Finally, realize that to turn that attack into your weapon you have to fall more in love with God than you are with the temptation or thing facing you. If it is a spiritual attack you are dealing with, you can turn that weapon against you into a sword in your hand by using that occasion to get closer and stronger in the Lord no matter what happens.

The Breakfast of Champions

Let me tell you how champions in God's army are supposed to function. God does not raise up champions so that they can be celebrities. He raises up champions so they can lead the charge for the army of God to go in and do the work. There are no "stars" in God's kingdom. We are all called to be kings and priests unto God, not to lord over each other.

Even Jesus said *"He who is greatest among you shall be your servant."* (Matthew 23:11) What did David do after he chopped off Goliath's head? No, he did not stop for a photo opportunity or an interview. David simply got out of the way so the rest of the army could go and fulfill its' purpose.

After Goliath's demise, the army of Israel then chased and conquered the fleeing Philistines. David did not go with the army to fight them. He only did his job which was to face the enemy, throw a stone, and use Goliath's own weapon to kill him.

All the Israelites needed was for their vision of victory to be restored and for the curses of fear and spectating to be broken. All they needed was a little encouragement to get up and attack the enemy like they should have forty days prior.

There were at least two things that kept David from going to fight the Philistines that day. Even though there was a great need for people to attack the fleeing enemy, David did not pursue. The first reason was David was humble enough and content enough with the victory over Goliath that he had nothing to prove. Therefore, he did not have to pursue the Philistines like the rest of the encampment.

The second reason was that he was able to recognize his abilities and his inabilities. As such, David did not try to do something for which he was not equipped nor qualified. At this point David did not yet have formal military training. That would come later when David was in Saul's court as his armorbearer and eventually as captain over a thousand.

Here in this valley David did not have the weapons, the armament, nor the ability to fight the entire army of the Philistines, or to even join in the pursuit with his countrymen. In verse 46 of I Samuel 17 David prophesied that he would feed the carcasses of the camp of the Philistines to the birds.

David knew that he was to only open the door for the army of Israel to fulfill their purpose and complete God's work. What could David have proved by defeating Goliath and then being killed in hand to hand combat with the Philistine army? Just because you opened the door does not mean that you are the one who is supposed to go through it.

Don't let the Lone Ranger ride again!
So why do we think that just because we are good at one thing we can do everything? You are not called to be the Lone Ranger. That is why we are all called to different things. Sometimes your job is to just open the door for others better suited to finish the work or to train another champion to fight.

How embarrassing it would be to try to open that door and be stopped by your big head getting stuck in the door jamb! Opening doors is not necessarily an ego builder. We all must work together doing the things God has called us to do. If you're not the champion to face Goliath, then find one who is.

If you are fighting battles as the "Lone Ranger" you will never have the reinforcements when you need them. Even the Lone Ranger had Tonto to help him. God did not intend for you to face your battles alone. Remember in a different context God said "...*It is not good that man should be alone*..." (Genesis 2: 18) Now do you see why it is so important to be part of an army, a local church?

Are you ready to rumble?
Look at the Goliaths you are facing in your life. You know what they are. Some of them you have helped to create. Others are just there because of Whose you are. Know that if you are submitted to God you are not in the battle alone. We already read in I Samuel 17: 47

that "the battle is the Lord's." You never know how God will use the trial you are facing now to give you the strength or the experience to defeat the Goliaths in your future or to get you closer to the fulfillment of your AC/PC.

Do you want to serve your enemy in bondage for the rest of your life? Are you going to continue to listen to the embarrassing cursing and bellowing day after day? Are you in the audience or in the army? How long will you wait for your purpose and dreams to fall out of the sky?

Get a vision for victory in your life. Develop a consistent relationship with God in prayer, praise, and His Word and become a faithful and meaningful part of a good Bible preaching church. Prepare for the fight like your life depends on it because guess what – IT DOES!

Chapter 14

Two Ways to Cause Success to Avoid You

Now when he had finished speaking to Saul, the soul of Jonathan was knit to the soul of David, and Jonathan loved him as his own soul. Saul took him that day, and would not let him go home to his father's house anymore. Then Jonathan and David made a covenant, because he loved him as his own soul. And Jonathan took off the robe that was on him and gave it to David, with his armor, even to his sword and his bow and his belt. So David went out wherever Saul sent him, and behaved wisely. And Saul set him over the men of war, and he was accepted in the sight of all the people and also in the sight of Saul's servants. Now it had happened as they were coming home, when David was returning from the slaughter of the Philistine, that the women had come out of all the cities of Israel, singing and dancing, to meet King Saul, with tambourines, with joy, and with musical instruments. So the women sang as they danced, and said: "Saul has slain his thousands, And David his ten thousands." Then Saul was very angry, and the saying displeased him; and he said, "They have ascribed to David ten thousands, and to me they have ascribed only thousands. Now what more can he have but the kingdom?" So Saul eyed David from that day forward. And it happened on the next day that the distressing spirit from God came upon Saul, and he prophesied inside the house. So David played music with his hand, as at other times; but there was a spear in Saul's hand. And Saul cast the spear, for he said, "I will pin David to the wall!" But David escaped his presence twice. Now Saul was afraid of David, because the LORD was with him, but had departed from Saul. Therefore Saul removed him from his presence, and made him his captain over a thousand; and he went out and came in before the people. And David behaved wisely in all his ways, and the LORD was with him. Therefore, when Saul saw that he behaved very wisely, he

was afraid of him. But all Israel and Judah loved David, because he went out and came in before them.
(I Samuel 18: 1 – 16)

So, you're well on your way now. You got your AC/PC (Anointing/Calling/Prophetic word/Personal Covenant) and the head of your adversary too! What's next? Well, you've been personally selected by the king to play at the palace and be at his side as his armor bearer. You're movin' on up to that de-luxe apartment in the sky! No more smelly unappreciative sheep. Hey, crowds of beautiful single women are singing your praises in the streets, literally! Glory to God, Hallelujah!!

What could be better? You are not resting on your laurels, but settling in the process until you are the king instead of the armor bearer, staying in the process until your true and total purpose is fulfilled. That was not easy or fun, but it was what David chose to do.

We begin this chapter immediately after David's defeat of Goliath, still in Saul's presence at the battlefront. In the previous three chapters of this book we compared how Saul and David dealt with Goliath. But what do you do after Goliath is dead and the crowd has gone home? Where do you go from there? How you deal with success is a critically important part of the process for fulfilling and maintaining your AC/PC and ultimately effectively realizing and implementing your true purpose.

Saul's humility was partially what attracted God to choose him as king. Yet Saul became so intoxicated with his throne that he allowed pride and power to consume him. **Saul lost his throne and negated his AC/PC by not properly dealing with success.** Do I have your attention yet? Don't repeat Saul's tragic mistake. Instead, learn from the failures and achievements of others as to how to deal with success.

To succeed or not to succeed, that is the question
Success is something that does not leave a person unchanged. Certainly success is not just limited to the accumulation of wealth or money. You do not have to be rich to be successful. Being poor

certainly does not mean you are automatically unsuccessful. You can be successful in your career, talents, skills, family, ministry, or any area in life and still deal with the same pitfalls that we will be discussing.

Everyone, with or without their permission, whether they like it or not, will be affected by success one way or another. How you deal with success will determine how much success you will ultimately achieve and sustain.

Are you frustrated in not achieving your goals or dreams? Does success often seem to elude you, always just in front of you but never quite close enough to hold onto for long? Are you always close enough to smell success but not close enough to taste it? I propose two reasons why this occurs: not having God's vision for your success and not properly dealing with the success you already have.

Reason One: Get God's vision for your success
First, maybe you never focused on God's vision of success for you. You say you can't do that? Having a vision for success is not selfish. It is required if you want to prosper. Where there is no vision, the people perish.

God's vision of success is for you to be able to aim your stone at your Goliath, knock him down, use his own sword to kill him, get out of the way for others to do their work, and then humbly accept your success without having to flaunt it. No photo opportunities, press conferences, or hero parades here. Just get up and faithfully and humbly execute the next assignment.

Specifically, if you have something you want to accomplish in life, don't wait for it to fall out of the sky. Don't even wait till you "feel" right about starting it. Look at where you are and where you would like to be. Then prayerfully map out the steps necessary to accomplish your goal and be open to the Lord changing your direction.

Often, once you start, Jesus will get you there faster than you ever imagined. But as the scripture says, *"Draw nigh to God, and He will draw nigh to you."* God will move, but He is waiting for you to take the first step towards your purpose and your success.

God's vision for your success is simple. He created you to be the head, and not the tail, to be above and not beneath. (Deuteronomy 28: 13) Why should you settle for less than what God has planned for you? *Beloved I wish above all things that thou mayest prosper and be in health, even as thy soul prospereth.* (III John 2 KJV)

God wants you to be successful in whatever you do, but for Christians it is directly related to our spiritual prosperity. If you don't believe me, then read Deuteronomy chapter 28.

God does not grant parade licenses. His provision for success doesn't mean you have a license to parade your blessings in front of everyone. It means that you will be blessed if you obediently and consistently stay in God's covenant for you.

And you shall remember the Lord your God, for it is He who gives you power to get wealth, that He may establish His covenant which he swore to your fathers, as it is this day. (Deuteronomy 8: 18)

In God's plan for your success there is no pressure or requirement for you to be the best, number one, the richest, the smartest, or the most handsome. You just have to be HIS. Insert your name in the blank space that follows:

For I know the thoughts that I think towards you _____, says the Lord, thoughts of peace and not of evil, to give you a future and a hope. (Jeremiah 29: 11)

It took me twenty years of being saved to figure out that God was on my side and that He wanted good things for me. Deceived, I used to think the Lord was always trying to humble me or punish me for my wrong actions. I thought that I would not receive blessings from God until I was humbled or had sufficiently suffered for my mistakes. I then became so distracted by my problems that I was debilitated from trying to achieve my goals, purpose, and dreams.

It's easy in life to run from problem to problem while struggling for success. But without a vision of what success is, you will only run from emergency to emergency without ever making any progress towards your goals and dreams. We become trapped by our problems and distracted by our daily life. Sometimes it seems that problems and emergencies are all that we face.

It's easy to forget about prayer, except when we need something. Don't get me wrong I am not trying to condemn anyone for praying when in need. Certainly that is the time to seek God earnestly. But what I challenge is when people come to God only to get their needs met and not for any other reason such as asking advice or giving God worship, praise, friendship, or love.

Did you know that if you only talk to God when you have needs, then you will probably stop talking to God when you do get the things you've been praying for? So what incentive does God have to answer your prayers quickly if He knows that as soon as you get what you want you will not pray as much? Ouch! (Yes, me too!)

God is not some great big order-taker in the sky. He wants to be your friend, one that sticks closer than a brother. (Proverbs 18: 24) He also wants to help you with your needs and be there to share in your successes. I know what you think of "friends" that only call you when they need something and are otherwise disinterested.

What should be your focus for success? If you become more interested in God than in yourself He will give you what you want. See what David wrote in Psalms 37: 4. *"Delight yourself also in the Lord, and He shall give you the desires of our heart."* The previously quoted scripture from Matthew tells us *"Seek first the kingdom of God and His righteousness, and all of these things shall be added unto you."*

Finally, to have a true grasp of God's success you have to finish what you have started. Remember how Jesus is described in Hebrews 12: 2 He is *"the author and the finisher of our faith."* He is the author, the originator, of our faith and He also finishes it.

I believe the word finish here is not only indicative of completion but also perfection, like finished cabinetry or the gemologist polishing a stone. Once finished, the wood is a work of art and the crude stone is a jewel. God does not just start something and then show up when it's done. He sticks with it through everything that occurs until it is complete and a vessel of honor and beauty. God finishes things and He expects us to do so as well. *"Whatever your hand finds to do, do it with your might."* (Ecclesiastes 9: 10)

Reason Two: If you can't handle what you got, how will you get more?

Secondly, and perhaps unknowingly more frequent, maybe you have not been faithful with the successes God has already given you, and He has delayed further success until you faithfully handle what you have.

Remember the scripture, *"He that is faithful in what is least is faithful in much."* (Luke 16: 10) What about *"For to everyone who has, more will be given, and he will have an abundance: but from him who does not have, even what he has will be taken away."* (Matthew 25: 29)

We have always used those scriptures to apply to finances, ability, responsibility, or ministry. But this important Biblical principle applies to the achieving and handling of success as well. If you can't properly handle the success you've achieved, then how can God trust you with more success? Let's now look at right and wrong ways to deal with success.

Chapter 15

Dealing With Success Without Driving Everybody Else Crazy

Let's look at the differences between how R.L. Pelshaw (hey, that's me!), Jonathan, and David dealt with success. We already know that Jonathan choked on success. Let me share with you my personal experiences with success.

I do not call my story a "testimony" because I would like to think that testimonies are something you are proud of or that you like to spread around. I am definitely not proud of the past behavior that I am about to relate. I present to you this account in the hope that as you achieve and maintain success you will recognize and avoid some of my stupid mistakes.

I, like Saul, initially dealt with success by becoming sickeningly and unknowingly puffed up with pride. Unfortunately for me and everybody else, it was not just a little bit of puffiness. I was so puffed up with it I could have been the official blow-fish of pride!

Jonathan's reaction was a little different. Success did not bring him satisfaction. His reaction to his success was such that he was immobilized from ever doing anything else great again.

David, on the other hand, reacted to success by following God's plan for achieving and dealing with success, which caused him to receive even more success from God.

How will you act when you finally get the desires of your heart? How will you act when you finally achieve the position, ministry, or possessions you want? Will you stop praying when all of your needs are met? Will you stop going to Sunday or Wednesday night service when your business or job starts to pay you the "big bucks?" Will you answer your own phone? Will you have the same friends? Will you have the same house or the same car? Will you be able to afford what you will buy then?

It's OK to have a nice car and a nice house if you have them in proper perspective. You should enjoy the things of this world as God created the world for us to enjoy. Just don't forget the God that blessed you with the success or the friends that helped you once you get there.

You say you won't forget your roots or the God that plucked you out of them? Remember the warning the Lord gave the children of Israel after He delivered them from bondage in Egypt.

Beware that you do not forget the Lord your God by not keeping His commandments, His judgments, and His statutes which I command you today, lest when you have eaten and are full, and have built beautiful houses and dwell in them; and when your flocks multiply, and your silver and gold are multiplied, and all that you have is multiplied: when your heart is lifted up, and you forget the Lord your God who brought you out of the land of Egypt, from the house of bondage: ... then you say in your heart, 'My power and the might of my hand have gained me this wealth...' Then it shall be if you by any means forget the Lord your God, and follow other gods, and serve them and worship them, I testify against you this day that you shall perish. (Deuteronomy 8: 11 – 14, 17, 19)

No one had a greater testimony than the children of Israel whom God triumphantly delivered from Egypt. Yet it did not take them long to forget God or the work that He did and start taking credit for it themselves. God blessed them with wealth and prosperity, but they eventually blew it by forgetting their source.

They forgot God in two ways. First they forgot to honor and thank God as their source of wealth, prosperity, and success. Secondly, even when they did thank God for what they had, they neglected to serve Him.

If I could just eat the crumbs that fall off the table
Remember the scripture we've quoted a few times that says the person who is faithful in little is faithful in much? Many people misread this scripture thinking that God wants to keep you with the "little." The Lord wants to make us faithful in the "little" so that He can trust us to not abuse, waste, or destroy the "much" He wants to release.

If you can't handle the small successes, what right do you have to complain that you are not getting the big successes? But I'm not talking about changes in your life. I'm concerned about the proper changes in your heart and your soul. God wants you to be blessed. He just wants you to remember Him once you get there.

Take the example from the Apostle Paul who said, *"I have learned to abound and to suffer need."* (Philippians 4: 12) Dealing with success is something that we must **learn**.

Have you considered that maybe the reason you have not yet fulfilled your purpose is because you have not shown God that you are mature or faithful enough to properly deal with the success He wants to give you? It may not be God who is delaying the realization of your dreams or purpose. The fact may be that you won't achieve major success in your life until you learn how to faithfully deal with the little successes you already have. I intimately know this truth from personal experience.

A really bad case of "Big Shot-Itis"
Laryngitis. Tonsillitis. Hepatitis. Bronchitis. These are some of the "itis" maladies you know and loathe. Even if you don't know what exactly what they are, you know they don't sound good. But bigshotitis? Never heard of that one you say? Well, I had it so bad I got to name it!

Bigshotitis is my name for what happens when, according to Romans 12: 3, a person thinks of himself "more highly than he ought." Bigshotitis is a unique affliction because it makes everyone but the person with it very sick. It is an easy disease for observers to readily diagnose, but almost impossible for those afflicted with it to detect.

Bigshotitis is a fancy name for good old fashioned pride, arguably the thing that God hates the most in the whole universe. Pride is what caused Lucifer's fall from heaven. (Isaiah 14: 12 - 20). Prov. 16:18 says, *"Pride goes before destruction, and a haughty spirit before a fall."* God hates pride so much that even the mere appearance of it is detestable in His sight and is the first thing listed in God's list of things that irritate Him the most.

These six things the LORD hates, Yes, seven are an abomination to Him: A proud look, a lying tongue, Hands that shed innocent blood, A heart that devises wicked plans, Feet that are swift in running to evil, A false witness who speaks lies, And one who sows discord among the brethren. (Proverbs 6: 16 – 19)

How do you get bigshotitis? In my opinion, it is no profound revelation to say that to become a bigshot first you have to want to be a bigshot. It may sound simple, but at one point or another, we have all been tempted, and probably fallen prey, to the allure of being a bigshot.

Another inroad for bigshotitis occurs when you do not have a grasp of reality or when you do not know and/or like who you are. I am not talking about mental delusion, maybe just unknowingly "thinking of yourself more highly than you ought" because you really are not happy with what you or your life is at the moment. I believe that is why God commands us to control our thoughts.

Casting down imaginations and every high thing that exalteth itself against the knowledge of God, and bringing into captivity every thought to the obedience of Christ. (II Corinthians 12: 5 KJV)

Specifically, I think bigshotitis develops like this. Remember earlier when I said that God puts in all of us a natural desire to be a champion? Everybody in one way or another has God-given goals, dreams, and visions for something great in life. I believe what occurs is that along with the natural God-given drives for success, the devil plants a weed seed in us to try to enable bigshotitis to get a foothold in our lives.

Unfortunately, it was easy for the weed seed of bigshotitis to get a stronghold in my life. I was not raised in a way to prepare me to be successful. My mother did the best job she could by herself with seven children living on welfare. Like an increasing number of single parent households, I never had anybody around to tell me that I could be successful, to teach me a vision for success, or to demonstrate the life and character that causes and maintains success.

To me, success was only what I observed on TV and in the world around me. Being a visual creature, I only saw the clothes, money, houses, cars, and lifestyle that I thought successful people had. This, of course, was radically different than the reality I had while growing up. What I did not see was the preparation, work, character, consistency, discipline, and dedication required to attain and maintain those things that I associated with success. At that time I foolishly thought the only way to have success was to have money.

Because of my lack of knowledge, I just did not know better. I did not know about the need for higher education to be able to get a good job to earn more money. No one taught me how to balance a checkbook, live on a budget, build and protect credit, develop a savings/investment plan, or do any of the other things that bring and maintain financial success. I was not taught that you accumulate wealth by living within your means so that you could save and invest money.

The only life I knew was to spend whatever money I had until it was gone. Believe me, no one had to force me to do this either. I liked spending money! God was going to bless me and meet my needs so what did I have to worry about if I wastefully scattered all of my seed, spent all of my money, right? He blessed me with the money for me to enjoy, so why not? That argument didn't work for the prodigal son that wasted his inheritance (Luke 15: 11 - 32), and unfortunately, it only caused me to unknowingly increase my own sorrows.

I had no one to teach me the discipline to say no to my own selfish appetites. I had no one to teach me how to be a champion in this area of my life. As such, I lacked the guidance and training to teach me how to deal with the success I could achieve if I tried and no one to teach me to be content while I was on the way to success. *"Godliness with contentment is great gain."* (I Timothy 6: 6)

Instead, even after becoming born-again, I was consumed with earning more so I could spend more and look more and more successful. Meanwhile, I was obliviously wasting enormous amounts of money and sowing weed-seeds that would quickly grow to haunt me.

The game is afoot.
Growing up I hated being poor so much that I fought and struggled so that I would never have to live in poverty. Even though I am the youngest of seven, I was the first in my family to conventionally graduate from high school and the first of my family to complete a college degree. I was also the first who went into the white collar work force.

After I started working I was blessed by God with favor and knowledge, and I started achieving success in my field of commercial real estate at the young age of twenty one, which was ten years after I met and started serving Jesus. I developed a strong drive and determination that initially brought me success, but it was improperly focused. Because of my Bigshotitis, I lacked the character, discipline, and maturity to properly deal with the success the Lord blessed me with at the time.

Drive and determination are good. But the character and consistency to maintain success are just as important, if not more important than the drive and determination used to get there. I unknowingly allowed my drive to achieve to consume my life to the point that I did not

have a clear grasp of reality or how sickening my Bigshotitis became to everyone around me. I had too much yeast of pride in the dough of my life, and it overpowered me.

Even before I had achieved the income and things I wanted, I lived in a fantasy world that had little correlation to real life. I always thought it was OK to "fake it till you make it." Was I ever wrong! But I was so consumed with improving the appearance of the status of my life that it blinded my view of reality. I was living way beyond my means which forced me to make unethical decisions, lie, cheat, and steal to support the lifestyle which I wanted.

Face the Consequences
Then bad things started to happen in my life. Because I was living a larger lifestyle than I should have, I could not afford all of the credit card debt I rapidly accumulated trying to look like a bigshot. Later, my own intoxication with pride caused me to enter a business relationship I was not prepared for professionally, financially, spiritually, or morally.

Because of my shortcomings, this venture disastrously folded. About that time I had already lived eight months in my house without water service because I could not pay the utility bills. Later that same year, at the ripe young age of twenty two, I surrendered my first house in lieu of foreclosure and moved back home with my mom. Talk about a quick way to deflate your ego!

Of course because I was not willing to take responsibility for my actions, I blamed all these bad things as attacks from the devil against me. I was saved, spirit-filled, a faithful supporter of my church, and the recipient of numerous prophecies of financial success. In addition I had my own AC/PC (Anointing/Calling/Prophetic word/Personal Covenant) so how could I be wrong? It had to be the devil's fault.

Actually, I was giving satan too much credit. He did not specially attack me. He did lay a trap for me that I was too dumb to notice. Yet I caused my own problems, and I gave the devil credit for them. The devil just knew how to shuffle my actions to tempt me to do the things that eventually caused my own downfall.

My liberty as a born-again Christian, my faithful church attendance, my big offerings, my prayers, and my Bible knowledge did not give me any special license to do whatever I wanted. I still had to deal with the crop I reaped from the seeds that were sown by my bigshotitis I had by not knowing how to properly deal with success.

Specifically, my actions and intoxication by pride invited the devil to plant the evil seeds that grew into the crop that I reaped. Heathens and saints alike know the scripture that says you reap what you sow. (Galatians 6: 7) All the devil did was keep watering the weed seeds of pride in my life that I allowed to be sown, and when they grew they yielded destructive fruit.

Since "pride goes before destruction," I should not have been surprised about the consequences I faced from my bigshotitis. After I lost my first business in 1989 at the age of twenty two, I went from making over $40,000 a year to making $5 an hour. I found despite my knowledge and achievements, it was almost impossible for me to get a job in my field because of the bad reputation I created for myself by my bigshotitis.

Consequences to bigshotitis are many and are not always financial. Among them, bigshotitis gives you a false sense of security that will impair you from making good decisions. Eventually bigshotitis can become so repulsive that it can cause you to lose jobs, promotions, spouses, friends, and even business or ministry opportunities. Look at what Saul's bigshotitis cost him: his AC/PC, his kingdom, his family, and even his own life.

For me, I thank God that He did not let me stay in that defeated position suffering the continued consequences of bigshotitis. He does not try to humble you, but that does not mean that He won't let you stay down long enough for you to get sick of something. Yes, you reap what you sow, but when you turn to Jesus He will pull that weed and the whole root system right out of your life so that it never affects you again!

As soon as I repented, the Lord restored me better than I was before despite all of the mistakes I caused. Jesus was just waiting for me to decide I would serve Him instead of my own agenda. I have since continued fighting bigshotitis, and it is a battle that with God's help I will continue to win.

If you have a touch of bigshotitis, or your cup runneth over with it, just ask God to give you a dose of His grace and to give you discernment to recognize when bigshotitis is influencing you. Then, just do the right thing!

You'll know them by their fruit.
Some of the fruits and symptoms of bigshotitis include:

- Always trying to impress or prove something to those around you
- Being too concerned with what people think about you
- Being unconcerned about the impact of your actions on others
- Competing and posturing for attention, being selfish and self-centered
- Bragging about your accomplishments, possessions, who you know, or what you have done
- Assuring your accomplishments, possessions, contacts, or knowledge are brought up in your conversations whether they have any relevance or not
- Exaggerating or even lying
- Criticizing other people so you look better
- Being unable to accept criticism and taking criticism too personally
- Being prone to bossiness
- Being prone to anger, resentment, or cruelty when you do not get your way or are not treated as you feel you should be
- Resenting when you are not selected or do not receive something you feel you deserve
- Thinking you are the only one with the right answers or the right method, having to get the last word in
- Having difficulty accepting help, presents, or blessings from others
- Having material things that you may not be able to afford just so you can maintain a perceived status
- Having a false sense of invincibility that impairs normal judgment

- Never being content with where or who you are, or what you have.

This list was not the result of research or data analysis. It was created from my own experience with bigshotitis.

Bigshotitis sets in when we lose proper perspective of ourselves, our goals, dreams, or visions and when we think we can do it all ourselves without the help or advice of anyone else. I think the first sprouts of bigshotitis usually occur when the success you have waited for starts to be realized. Sometimes even the slightest hint of success, either real, emerging, or fabricated, can be enough to cause you to become intoxicated with yourself and your status.

Instead of being infatuated with God Who is trying to fulfill your dreams, we make ourselves, our position, our possessions, our gifts/anointings, or our success an idol that we unknowingly worship more than we worship God.

Everybody has areas in life where they are vulnerable to bigshotitis. Oral Roberts warns preachers to beware of the "Three G's: Gold, Glory, and Girls." A small case of bigshotitis is usually limited to a few areas, where a severe case of bigshotitis can consume and make inroads into how you behave in every area of life. But any and all fruits of bigshotitis can and will have severe negative impact in your life if left unchecked. It's literally like a weed that will choke the life out of all the good crop if you don't kill it soon.

Don't get drunk on yourself
I like to compare the process of acquiring bigshotitis to getting intoxicated. First you start with a sip, and it has little effect on you. Everybody else is drinking too so it must be OK. Now you have enjoyed your first drink and with little effect you feel it is safe to sip a little more. You keep drinking so that with each drink you unknowingly become less and less in control until you are totally intoxicated.

Intoxication dulls your senses, impairs your vision and judgment, can be life threatening to yourself and others, and makes you stink to everybody around you. But with bigshotitis, the "drink" you get drunk on is yourself.

And be not drunk with wine, wherein is excess; but be filled with the Spirit. (Ephesians 5: 18 KJV)

Why are we discussing bigshotitis in a book about the life of David? If David had not properly dealt with the success achieved over Goliath, he would have never been invited to Saul's court. If David had bigshotitis he would have never survived the process to become King. He would have repulsed all of the people that were supposed to come help him along the way. Saul's servants and the other soldiers would not have favored or honored him. He would have never been accepted by the people, and later the elders of Judah would never have asked him to be king.

We must deal with success before we get the fulfillment of our AC/PC. Improperly dealing with success will remove you once you get there, or even keep you from ever getting it at all.

I'll just wait for God to humble me.
OK, I've convinced you, and now you want bigshotitis out of your life. We'll just wait on the Lord and let Him deal with it when and how He wants to, right? NO!!

Take a look at the first part of James 4: 10."*Humble **yourselves** in the sight of the Lord.*" (emphasis added) We are commanded to humble ourselves, not wait for humility to hit us in the head while mystically descending from heaven. You are going to have to use your God-given common sense and discipline to make decisions, guard conversation, think thoughts, and live your life in a manner to cause you to "humble yourself."

I used to think that sometimes bad things happened to me because God was trying to humble me. God does not try to humble anybody. That is not His nature. How do I know? Look at the relationship between God and the devil.

God did not try, nor is He now trying, to humble satan. We know from scripture that the sole reason of satan's expulsion from heaven was his pride. God flung satan out of Heaven because He is a perfect sinless Being that can have no part with sin. Yet despite all the pride of satan and how much God hates pride, the Lord does not try to humble the devil, and He is not trying to humble you either. Why would He attempt to do something that He commanded and empowered you yourself to do?

Look at all of James 4:10. *"Humble yourselves in the sight of the Lord **and He will lift you up**."* Why would a God that is trying to humble you and keep you down say that He would lift you up if you humble yourself in His sight? God will not humble you, humiliate you, make you suffer, or try to "take you down a few pegs." He will, and wants to, lift you up if you humble yourself to Him. The key is the humbling of yourself "in His sight."

Appearance and approval of others has no connection to being humble in the sight of God. Humility in God's sight is what He sees in your heart when there is no audience. Being humble in the sight of God is yielding to His plan and purpose regardless of your opinion, reaction, feelings, or how it makes you look in the eyes of man.

We all want God to lift us up, but are we ready to humble ourselves in His sight in order to get exalted? Stop wasting time by waiting for God to do something that you need to do. Remember how pride comes before destruction? Get yourself humble before it's too late. To do that simply apply the following principle.

But He gives more grace. Therefore He says: "God resists the proud, But gives grace to the humble." Therefore submit yourself to God, resist the devil and he will flee from you. Draw near to God, and He will draw near to you. Cleanse your hands, you sinners, and purify your hearts you double-minded. (James 4: 6-8)
Seek God to give you grace and strength to change, and then walk it out. Repeat as necessary until conquered.

Did you ever try to walk a tightrope?
What about when it seems like you're "walking it out" under difficult circumstances? Maintaining a proper balance between bigshotitis and humility is sometimes as difficult as walking a tightrope in gale-force wind with life or death consequences.

We all want recognition for a job well done. But at what point does our desire for recognition go farther than it should? God gave us hopes and dreams we should strive for, but we must maintain a balance between properly dealing with success and the avoidance of bigshotitis.

God wants you to succeed and prosper. He just doesn't want you to be consumed with it. It's OK to be confident and self assured, as long as that is not a mask for self glorification. It's great to share good news, but ask yourself if that person really has to know, or even why you're talking about something before it even comes out of your lips. Is what you have to say glorifying to God or is it consciously or unconsciously feeding bigshotitis?

Maintaining a proper perspective of success and bigshotitis is not a matter of what you say. It is a matter of what the purpose in your heart was for your actions. Success is something God wants for all of His children. It comes through observing His Word.

*This book of the Law shall not depart from your mouth, but you shall meditate in it day and night, that you may observe to do according to all that is written in it. For then you will make your way prosperous, and then you shall have **good success**. (emphasis added) (Joshua 1: 8)*

What is true humility?
Religion has taught us that humility is to live in an impoverished lowly state. But what is it really? You can be successful and humble. We are commanded to be like God and His nature is certainly not of pride. Yet He is the wealthiest and most successful Being that ever will be in this universe. Everything that He does succeeds. He's never wrong. He's always on time.

The Lord is described in many scriptures as being "high and lifted up," not lowly and decrepit. We are His children and His heirs. If we're to "reign with Him," (Revelations 20: 6) we better get a perspective of how we are supposed to act in the throne room.

True humility is the ability to enjoy the things that Jesus blesses you with without forgetting that He was the Source of them and without letting bigshotitis get a hold in your life.

I have heard it said that "Pride is thinking of yourself more than you ought. Humility is thinking and saying what God says about you."

I do not apologize for my success, anointing, education, talent, possessions, or the other things God has blessed me with. Because I want to humble myself to the Lord so He will exalt me, I do not flaunt the Lord's blessings to anyone. That does not mean that I try to hide them. It means I do not have to, nor should I ever, parade them in front of people.

I think Jesus sums up how we should act in the principles exemplified in Luke 14: 8 – 11

When you are invited by anyone to a wedding feast, do not sit down in the best place, lest one more honorable than you be invited by him and he who invited you and him come and say to you, 'Give place to this man,' and then you begin with shame to take the lowest place. But when you are invited, go and sit down in the lowest place, so that when he who invited you comes he may say to you, 'Friend, go up higher.' Then you will have glory in the presence of those who sit at the table with you. ***For whoever exalts himself will be humbled, and he who humbles himself will be exalted.*** (emphasis added)

How to let the air out

There are two ways to let the air out of a balloon. You can pop the balloon or you can untie the knot and let the air out in a controlled fashion that is not destructive to the balloon. If you have been the "blowfish of pride" like I was, how do you want God to let the hot air of bigshotitis out of your life? Do you want the destruction that comes from the popping of pride or do you want God to give you the grace to expel bigshotitis from your life?

I thank God that He mercifully let the air of bigshotitis out of me. I had it in me until I called on Jesus to give me the grace and strength to get it out of me.

The worst part of bigshotitis is the emptiness and pain experienced when you realize you are not the richest, smartest, best-looking, or the most talented. Unfortunately for those of us who have suffered from bigshotitis, it hurts when someone shows up that has more or is better than you. The truth of the matter is, eventually someone will always come along that can out do you. If your self-worth and identity are connected to being the best or the most, when someone greater comes along it will painfully and quickly "pop your balloon."

Do not create a situation for yourself that will eventually end in a dramatic consequence like the popped balloon. Realize that you should not allow bigshotitis to work through you, even after you achieved success, because someone will always and eventually materialize that has more money, more success, more talent, more friends, more education, or more of the thing that has been feeding your bigshotitis.

Chapter 16

Success Without Bigshotitis – What To Do When You Get There

In many ways, we all see bits of ourselves in David's life. I can relate to the fact that I did not have an abundance of parental encouragement. I wonder if David ever resented the fact that all of the family was with the prophet Samuel, and he was stuck with the sheep?

The initial exclusion of David at the sacrifice with Samuel proves the point that no one thought he had the potential to be great. Yet with his facing of Goliath, we can all admire the underdog winning against impossible odds.

David's victory that day was not to prove to the people that didn't believe in him that he had purpose. David's success against Goliath was to prove to God that he could be trusted to implement his AC/PC with faithfulness and honor before the Lord. David did not know it, but it was to prove to God that he could be trusted with success. Therefore, the Lord was willing to give him more.

Having suffered from bigshotitis myself, I have tremendous respect for David because when he became the overnight national hero, he did not allow it to go to his head. Even when the women were singing in the streets, David reacted properly to success. I know from past experience that I probably would not have handled those situations as well as David.

I wonder what thoughts were going through David's mind as the King's son was giving him his personal effects and a personal covenant of friendship? Do you think David called home to tell everybody about the women parading in the streets or the fact that he was now the king's son's best friend? Do you think when David came into a room that he had to mention that he defeated Goliath? Did David proclaim "make way for the king's armor bearer?" I doubt it.

Everybody sees the rewards of success, but we quickly forget about the pain and sacrifice required to achieve and maintain success. Don't be deceived into thinking that everything will be all right once you get promoted or earn a little more money. David's real problems did not occur until he stepped out to walk in the AC/PC that God gave him. His life was real easy before he was thrust into the uphill climb of fulfilling his purpose.

Did you hear the one about ...?
And it happened on the next day that the distressing spirit from God came upon Saul, and he prophesied inside the house. So David played music with his hand, as at other times; but there was a spear in Saul's hand. And Saul cast the spear, for he said, "I will pin David to the wall!" But David escaped his presence twice. Now Saul was afraid of David, because the LORD was with him, but had departed from Saul. (I Samuel 18: 10 – 12)

Do you think God has a sense of humor? I do. Look at the way He created you! For a bigger laugh, look at the way He created me! Through my desire to understand an obscure portion of scripture, the Lord revealed a little bit of His sense of humor to me.

Verse 10 in the King James version of I Samuel 18 says that an *"evil spirit from God came upon Saul, and he prophesied in the midst of the house."* I came across this scripture when I was teaching my Sunday School series on the life of David. This scripture bothered me and did not make sense to me. I consulted a few Bible commentaries and talked to some friends but I could not make any sense of this passage. To me, how could an evil spirit come from God? I know that Saul had been gifted with the ability to prophesy, but how could he prophesy with an evil spirit? Was what he said in the prophesy true or false?

I fasted and prayed for direction and understanding from God, and this is what I received concerning my questions.

I believe that the evil spirit sent by God was jealousy that the Lord had allowed to come upon Saul. Saul had accurately prophesied by the Spirit of God in the past. But since the gift of God is without repentance (Romans 11: 29), Saul was indeed truly and accurately prophesying what God wanted him to say, even with jealousy. I would love to know exactly what was said that day. Since Samuel already pronounced judgment that Saul would lose his throne, the only thing that Saul could accurately prophesy was something I will hypothesize to be something like this:

> *David, I am sitting on this throne, but I have been removed as being king. Unlike me, an old, crusty, selfish, blowhard has-been, you are God's true anointed king, and a man after His own heart, and soon you will sit here on this throne instead of me.*

I theorize Saul became so angry about the words that came out of his own lips that he twice tried to kill David for it! In an ironic way, that's funny! The irony is the great ruling king was saying this to a brave bright-eyed kid that just a few days before was protecting sheep. You know the ventriloquist and the dummy? Imagine God coming down in the midst of David and Saul and taking control so that Saul becomes the dummy that speaks what God wants him to say. That to me, although tragic, shows God's sense of humor. Not that this was a matter to be joked about, but rather that God is so much in control that He can take a great king sitting on a throne and make him do stupid things.

The sad thing is that Saul didn't get the joke. Instead of yielding and preserving his life, he became intent on ignoring God until it was too late. My advice to you: don't become the brunt of God's jokes. Submit completely to His plan before it is too late.

Why can't we all just get along?
I have had some tough bosses, but never have I had one that literally tried to kill me. I am sure I probably drove many of my old bosses and others to at least think about killing me though! Fortunately, I have never had to face a literal attempt on my life.

What about David? Yes, it was great that David was now in the royal court ministering to the king. But who would want that job after you figured out that it included putting up with Saul's mood swings and constant javelin throwing?

And what about the ladies singing in the streets? Of course they would sing and dance for David, the hero who was single and good looking. He was a great catch, certainly Israel's most eligible bachelor, unlike Saul who was old and married. The ladies' reports of David "killing ten thousands" were greatly exaggerated, because David only killed one, Goliath, not the thousands the ladies gave him credit for. Actually, the ladies were trying to give David credit for the victory of the army, the whole team that pursued and slaughtered the Philistines that day.

Saul should have been mature enough to recognize the exaggerated account of the ladies was not true and was probably made to try to impress and attract David. Moreover, Saul should have been mature enough and secure enough in his position as king to allow the hero the recognition and appreciation due him. If Saul really wanted people singing for him in the streets, he should have strapped on his own armor and faced Goliath forty days before David showed up.

After the ladies sang David's praise in the streets, it says in verse 9 of II Samuel 18 that *"Saul eyed David from that day forward."* Have you ever been "eyed" by someone? That's when they look at and magnify every aspect of your life with a predisposition to find a negative thing to discredit you. Yet despite Saul's tireless efforts, because of the AC/PC on David's life and the integrity and consistency in which David lived, Saul could find no fault in David.

Here Saul had a dilemma. Saul loved David's gifts, anointings, and the victories he made for him. Yet Saul was afraid of the very anointing and success in David that he benefited from.

Saul should not have tried to hinder or hold down David. In his lifetime Saul only benefited from David's success. See why we should raise up champions? Let them succeed. It only helps you.

Despite this, Saul became threatened by his subordinate and took conscious measures to try to hurt him.

Verse 13 of II Samuel 18 indicates that Saul removed David from being his armor bearer and made him a captain over a thousand. Rather, God moved him into this position to teach him how lead and train soldiers. Here David continued the development process to cause him to grow into his destiny as King.

At the time of the job change David might have thought it was a demotion going from armor bearer to captain over a thousand. Again, what the devil meant for evil, God meant for good. While David was working among the men, it says he:

[W]ent out and came in before the people. And David behaved wisely in all his ways, and the LORD was with him. Therefore, when Saul saw that he behaved very wisely, he was afraid of him. But all Israel and Judah loved David, because he went out and came in before them. (I Samuel 18: 13- 16)

David acted like a "regular guy" by going in and out before the people. He gained the love and respect of Israel and Judah by wisely, humbly, and faithfully working his job like everyone else without bigshotitis or special privileges.

The check is in the mail
Have you ever had someone owe you money that you had difficulty collecting? Or maybe you were like me and you have had times when you had difficulty paying what you owed. Maybe your payments were made but they were never on time. Maybe you heard or had to make excuses like "the check is in the mail" as to why the money wasn't there on time or even at all.

Earlier we noted that Saul promised wealth, tax exemption, and his daughter to the champion of Goliath. Yet read between the lines of this passage, particularly verses 18 and 23 noted here.

Then Saul said to David, "Here is my older daughter Merab; I will give her to you as a wife. Only be valiant for me, and fight the Lord's battles." For Saul thought, "Let my hand not be against him, but let the hand of the Philistines be against him." So David said to Saul, "Who am I, and what is my life or my father's family in Israel, that I should be son-in-law to the king?" But it happened at the time when Merab, Saul's daughter, should have been given to David, that she was given to Adriel the Meholathite as a wife. Now Michal, Saul's daughter, loved David. And they told Saul, and the thing pleased him. So Saul said, "I will give her to him, that she may be a snare to him, and that the hand of the Philistines may be against him." Therefore Saul said to David a second time, "You shall be my son-in-law today." And Saul commanded his servants, "Communicate with David secretly, and say, 'Look, the king has delight in you, and all his servants love you. Now therefore, become the king's son-in-law.'" So Saul's servants spoke those words in the hearing of David. And David said, "Does it seem to you a light thing to be a king's son-in-law, seeing I am a poor and lightly esteemed man?"

In this passage of scripture, Saul secretly enticed David to become his son-in-law. David's response was that he could not be the king's son-in-law because he was poor and lightly esteemed. If Saul kept his promise to David about his reward for killing Goliath, David would have been wealthy enough to pay a dowry, which would have been unnecessary anyway since Saul had promised his daughter to the victor of Goliath.

Verse 19 records that Saul had given Merab, his eldest daughter, to another man, even though he gave his word to give her to David. Here Saul steals from David by not keeping his word. David calls himself poor, so he evidently did not get the reward for killing Goliath.

You can't keep a good man down.
Then Saul said, "Thus you shall say to David: 'The king does not desire any dowry but one hundred foreskins of the Philistines, to take vengeance on the king's enemies.'" But Saul thought to make David fall by the hand of the Philistines. So when his servants told David

these words, it pleased David well to become the king's son-in-law. Now the days had not expired; therefore David arose and went, he and his men, and killed two hundred men of the Philistines. And David brought their foreskins, and they gave them in full count to the king, that he might become the king's son-in-law. Then Saul gave him Michal his daughter as a wife. Thus Saul saw and knew that the LORD was with David, and that Michal, Saul's daughter, loved him; and Saul was still more afraid of David. So Saul became David's enemy continually. Then the princes of the Philistines went out to war. And so it was, whenever they went out, that David behaved more wisely than all the servants of Saul, so that his name became highly esteemed.

The demotion and the failure to pay his promised reward does not stop David either. He sticks with Saul through thick and thin. Unlike many of us who would have walked immediately once we did not receive our check, David did not run from his appointed task despite the setbacks.

So what does Saul do next? He goes to another plan to coerce David into a suicide mission that will destroy him. Saul again manipulates the situation to attempt to solve his perceived problem. He does not want to harm David himself, but he concocts a scheme to bring him into destruction.

David should have known when Saul did not initially keep his word that he should not have entered into any agreement with Saul, particularly one that Saul controlled. David knew not to negotiate on the enemy's terms, but David did not consider Saul his enemy, despite the fact that later *"Saul became David's enemy continually."* David probably took Saul's suggestion just so he could be submissive to the will of his king.

Despite Saul's attempted trap, David successfully fulfills the dowry requirements and gains even more favor and respect from the people and more opposition from Saul.

Here's the heart of the matter
David was able to endure the struggles and conflicts while he was walking towards his purpose, the fulfillment of his AC/PC. For more insight into the heart of David, please read Psalm 27 that shortly follows.

More than his kingdom, his call, or his dreams, David wanted to dwell with God first, to behold His beauty, to bask in the wonderful presence of his Lord, his Savior, and his friend. If this book has done anything, I hope to have challenged you to enhance your personal relationship with God, and to help focus, motivate, and strengthen you in finding and fulfilling your purpose.

PSALMS 27

The LORD is my light and my salvation; Whom shall I fear? The LORD is the strength of my life; Of whom shall I be afraid? When the wicked came against me To eat up my flesh, My enemies and foes, They stumbled and fell. Though an army may encamp against me, My heart shall not fear; Though war should rise against me, In this I will be confident. One thing I have desired of the LORD, That will I seek: That I may dwell in the house of the LORD All the days of my life, To behold the beauty of the LORD, And to inquire in His temple. For in the time of trouble He shall hide me in His pavilion; In the secret place of His tabernacle He shall hide me; He shall set me high upon a rock. And now my head shall be lifted up above my enemies all around me; Therefore I will offer sacrifices of joy in His tabernacle; I will sing, yes, I will sing praises to the LORD. Hear, O LORD, when I cry with my voice! Have mercy also upon me, and answer me. When You said, "Seek My face," My heart said to You, "Your face, LORD, I will seek." Do not hide Your face from me; Do not turn Your servant away in anger; You have been my help; Do not leave me nor forsake me, O God of my salvation. When my father and my mother forsake me, Then the LORD will take care of me. Teach me Your way, O LORD, And lead me in a smooth path, because of my enemies. Do not deliver me to the will of my adversaries; For false witnesses have risen against me, And such as breathe out violence. I would have lost heart, unless I had believed That I would see the goodness of the LORD In the land of the living. Wait on the LORD; Be of good courage, And He shall strengthen your heart; Wait, I say, on the LORD!

Chapter 17

So What Have We Learned From David?

We all have God-given dreams and desires. Sometimes God will birth those dreams and desires inside of you. Other times He may use a prophet or a spiritual leader to impart them to you like He used Samuel to impart the AC/PC to David. Once the AC/PC was received, David did not try to walk into the throne room. He knew he would have to work at making himself ready for his purpose.

David did not just sit around and wait for his throne to fall out of the sky. He faithfully and humbly executed each task before him until God placed him on the path towards his destiny. After receiving his AC/PC, there was nothing David could do to effect the realization of his purpose. He went back to what he was doing before until the Lord opened doors for him to walk through.

Without any planning or special preparation David was thrust into a situation where he was witnessing the humiliation and shame Goliath was causing God's people. Aware of his gifts, abilities, shortcomings, and the AC/PC given by God, David determined he would face Goliath and trust God to perform His word. Without trying to be anybody other than himself, he used his seemingly insignificant knowledge and skill, manifested in the sling and the stones, to knock down a formidable enemy. Then like God always wants us to do, David used what the enemy was attacking him with to destroy his foe.

Killing Goliath was a triumph, but David was not ready for the throne yet. True, the conquest welcomed him into the king's court, which is when his life just started to become difficult. At a time when he should have been enjoying life the most, David had to avoid the murder attempts his boss and king flung at him. David sacrificed everything in his service to Saul, yet Saul showed his appreciation by stealing his reward and trying to kill David for his successes.

David properly dealt with success. He did not despise it, hide it, or parade it in front of everyone. He was thankful for the success achieved, but he did not dwell on it. He simply focused on serving his king to the best of his abilities, even when his king tried to kill him for it.

Despite this very real opposition, David did not stop serving or obeying. He did not stop dreaming, preparing, or faithfully living his life. He persevered through the situation while the Lord ordered his steps. As we will explore in the next book of this series, ***Thriving Through the Wilderness***, David's steps later brought him to the brink of despair, loneliness, and hopelessness, and finally to his throne. The heart and character of David gave him the strength to achieve and succeed in his dreams and purpose.

By reading this book I hope you have greater insight into your own dreams and purpose, as well as recognize some of the strategies the devil will use to try to keep them from you. I hope you realize you are important to God, and that no matter how hopeless or frustrating your circumstances may look, God does have great plans for you. He is just waiting for you to seek Him first, so that He can add these other things to you. God has already selected you, now He waits for you to settle in His process of obedience and consistency so that He can mold and develop you into a great and wonderful purpose. He wants to prepare you for the success He has planned for you. How long will you keep Him waiting?

I am so thankful that God has a mechanism to realize the dreams and visions He gives us. He has made a way for each of us to raise up the champion that is already there inside us, and the other people in our life we influence. It's all up to you now. Where will YOU go from here?

P.S. – *You can do it!*

***Now thanks be to God
who always leads us to triumph in Christ...***
II Corinthians 2: 14a

ENDNOTES

[i] Bill Hamon, <u>Prophets and Personal Prophecy</u>, *Destiny Image*, Shippensburg, Pennsylvania (1989) p. 66

[ii] Bill Hamon, <u>Prophets, Pitfalls and Principles</u>, *Destiny Image*, Shippensburg, Pennsylvania (1991) p. 190

[iii] Terry Nance, <u>God's Armor Bearers</u>, *Harrison House,* Tulsa, Oklahoma (1990), pp. 17 – 27